Fish: Keeping & Breeding in Captivity

Piranhas

Prof. Manolito Pinkguni

Published in association with T.F.H. Publications, Inc.,
the world's largest and most respected publisher of pet literature

Chelsea House Publishers
Philadelphia

CONTENTS

Fish: Keeping & Breeding in Captivity

Aquarium Setting Up
Siamese Fighting Fish
Catfish
Goldfish
Guppies
Marine Aquarium
Piranhas
Tropical Fish
Angelfish

Publisher's Note: All of the photographs in this book have been coated with FOTOGLAZE™ finish, a special lamination that imparts a new dimension of colorful gloss to the photographs.

Reinforced Library binding & Super-Highest Quality Boards

This edition ©1999 TFH Publications, Inc., 1 TFH Plaza, Neptune City, NJ 07753. This special library bound edition is made expressly for Main Line Book Company a division of Chelsea House Publishers.

Library of Congress Cataloging-in-Publication Data applied for
0-7910-5093-9

Library of Congress Cataloging-in-Publication Data

Pinkguni, Manolito.
        Piranhas / Manolito Pinkguni.
                p. cm. — (fish and aquariums)
        Includes index.
        Summary: A guide to keeping piranhas with information about the physical characteristics of the different varieties, their care and feeding, and how to set up and maintain the aquariums in which they will make their home.
        ISBN 0-7910-5093-9 (hc)
        1. Piranhas--Juvenile literature. 2. Aquariums--Juvenile literature.
        (1. Piranhas. 2. Aquariums.) I. Title. II. Series.
        SF458.P57P55 1998
        639.3'748—dc21   98-23989
                                                           CIP
                                                           AC

INTRODUCTION

Although a number of fishes have gained notoriety in films, books, and television, two are blessed with especially unsavory reputations. These are the great white shark of "Jaws" fame and the piranhas of South America. You can't keep a shark in your aquarium, but the piranha you can. As with all animals that have gained infamous reputations, the reality is often somewhat less than the legend. This said, the notoriety of these fishes is no figment of the imagination. They are extremely dangerous and quite capable of doing exactly what they are famed for doing.

A school of piranhas can reduce a wounded crocodile to its skeleton in the time it would take to haul it out of the water on a length of rope! It would take even less time to devour a human being. However, these fishes are not swimming around South American waters seeking out humans and other mammals for dinner. If they were, no animal would ever venture into piranha infested waters. In this sense, therefore, they are rather misunderstood.

"Piranha" does not refer to a single species, as is often thought by the average person, but is a common name applied to a group of species, all of which are very closely related. Some are more dangerous than others. They are relatives of many of the most popular and peaceful fishes (tetras and the like) that are seen in the aquarium hobby, as you will learn in the following chapter.

Piranhas cannot be regarded as species to be recommended to the first time aquarist. Their diet and water requirements must be well suited to their needs. They will, once adult, require a large aquarium. Being carnivorous (and potentially savage) they cannot be kept with other fishes without the risk that they may either nip pieces from them or devour them. Indeed, they can only be reliably accommodated in the average home situation with their own kind and, even then, while they are juveniles. Even in this situation there will be the risk that some of them will be mutilated or eaten by their slightly larger or stronger tank mates.

They are, therefore, a collection of species supported in the aquarium hobby by a number of enthusiastic specialists. Often, they may be seen in a pet or aquarium store because their fame makes them an instant source of curiosity, thus an "attraction" for the stores that have them on display.

In the following chapters all of the information that you will need to know about piranhas from a hobbyist's point of view is detailed. If you then feel you would like to own a piranha you are advised to seek the advice of an enthusiast, or a store manager that is experienced with them, before venturing any further.

You will not, of course, ever be housing a collection of them in a single aquarium (this would have to be an enormous tank), but even so you are cautioned that even a single fish can inflict a severe injury to a hand or finger carelessly placed into the water. These are not the sort of fishes you should obtain on a passing "whim," no more than you would obtain a poisonous snake, or spider, just to say you owned one. Given due respect for the potential of what their dental work can do and proper care to their needs, piranhas are an interesting group of fishes that will always command attention and have a nucleus of serious devotees.

PHOTO BY DR. KARL KNACK.

Juvenile *Serrasalmus nattereri*. These are probably the most popular piranhas and most prevalent in the Amazon River system.

WHAT ARE PIRANHAS?

There are about 20,000 species of fishes living in the various waters of our planet. There are more fishes than all the other vertebrate animals (mammals, birds, reptiles, and amphibians) put together. As all life evolved in the water, and most of our planet's surface is covered by water, this is perhaps not surprising. It is most probable that there are still a few thousand fishes yet to be discovered.

A fish may be broadly defined as an animal that lives in water, breathes via gills throughout its life, moves by means of fins, has a body supported by a backbone, has a covering of scales (some have secondarily lost them), and whose body temperature is controlled by the environment (poikilothermic, meaning variable, but commonly known as cold-blooded) rather than internally (homoiothermic, meaning the same temperature, or warm-blooded). Using this definition, whales, dolphins, and their like are not fishes (they are mammals), nor are many of the other creatures you can find living in water that sport the name (ex. starfishes, cuttlefishes).

Over 90% of all fishes are bony, as compared with the sharks, rays, skates, and the like in which bone is replaced by cartilage. There are also a number of jawless fishes. The bony fishes are all placed in a group (class) called Osteichthyes. This is divided into many groups (orders) in which the member species have a number of common features that warrant their being grouped together. One of these orders is the Characiformes. Within this order are many famous aquarium fishes, such as the anostomins and leporinins (family Anostomidae), the hatchetfishes (family Gasteropelecidae), the pencilfishes (family Lebiasinidae), the distichodontins (family Distichodontidae), and the very extensive list of tetras, the many species that carry the name characin, and those that are the subject of this book, the piranhas (family Characidae). Although the name characin is generally reserved for the family Characidae, it has also been used extensively for species that are allocated to other families of this order. The infamous piranhas have sometimes also been housed in their own family, Serrasalmidae, but most recently are considered as being included in the subfamily Serrasalminae within the family Characidae. In the subfamily Serrasalminae are included two major groups, the basic plant eaters (*Colossoma*, *Metynnis*, etc.), which total about seven genera with about 60 species, and the piranhas (also known as the caribs) proper, with four genera (*Serrasalmus*, *Pygocentrus*, *Pygopristes*, and *Pristobrycon*) and about 50 or so species, many of which are still to be

PHOTO BY GLEN SCOTT AXELROD.

Dried piranhas with beads for eyes are a typical souvenir sold in the Amazon. The fish are caught, soaked in formalin, rinsed and then dried. They are mounted on Amazonian hardwoods, painted, varnished and sold to tourists.

described. Many of these piranhas are not dangerous, but it is the few that are that give them all their evil reputation. The classification of these fishes is discussed in more detail in the chapter on the individual species.

DISTRIBUTION & HABITAT

Characins and their allies (of which there are over 1,300 species) are found mainly in Central and South America, with only about 200 species native to African waters. In evolutionary terms, they are thought to

dangerous to humans when living in tributaries and waters that become cut off from the main river during dry periods. When this happens, and they have devoured most of the available fishes that form the greater part of their natural diet, they will of course attack anything that will satiate their at times ravenous appetites. However, like many fishes, piranhas can endure quite long periods without feeding, and many of them survive these periods of drought to return to the main river following heavy

PHOTO BY DR. HERBERT R. AXELROD.

This huge *Serrasalmus notatus* was caught in the Brazilian village of the Caiapo Indians in October, 1964. The fish was 19 inches (about 50 cm) long. It is doubtful that the village or the large piranhas exist any more.

have existed as a group for maybe up to 150 million years in the case of the earliest types, with the division into African and American forms occurring about 90 million years ago. The piranhas are found only in northern South America (the Amazon, Orinoco, Paraguay, and San Francisco river systems as well as in the rivers of the Guianas), but most are indigenous to the great Amazon basin. They live in many rivers and their tributaries, as well as within lakes.

Piranhas are possibly at their most

seasonal storms.

Only when mammals (which include humans) are wounded do the more ferocious species smell the blood and attack. Most of the gory stories you hear about them are straight from the imagination of novelists and script writers but, this said, they clearly remain potentially among the most savage and dangerous of all freshwater fish species.

There is no doubt that a number of people have been killed by these fishes—but this is a fact that can be said of hundreds of animal species. Indeed, there are dozens of animals that kill more people every year than piranhas have accomplished over many decades, yet these fishes have been elevated to a status that has no relationship to its real threat to humans.

Basic Anatomy

The piranha is a typical fish with comparable anatomy, but it does have certain features not always seen in all fishes. Of course they do have the dentistry that is related to their mode of feeding. I cannot discuss anatomy in any detail, so what follows is a basic overview.

Shape & Size: Depending on the species, piranhas are discus to rhomboid

Serrasalmus striolatus.

Serrasalmus elongatus collected in the Lago Las Pupunhas on the Rio Madeira. It was 12 inches (30 cm) long.

in shape, being strongly laterally compressed. A few species, such as *Serrasalmus elongatus*, are atypical in that, as the name suggests, they have a more elongate shape. Size again depends on the species involved, the larger examples reaching 40cm (22in), with 22-31cm (8.5-12in) being a typical length for most species once they are adult. This fact should be taken under advisement very carefully before these fishes are considered for the home aquarium.

In broad terms there is a shape distinction between those species that are held to be very dangerous and those that are less so. The dangerous species have a more rounded head profile compared to the less dangerous species

in which a dip or indentation can be seen above the eyes. The jaw muscles of the dangerous species are also larger and more powerful.

Color: Piranhas cannot be regarded as very colorful fishes. The range is from silver through blue-green to brown, with many sporting spots or bars on their sides, others having some red on the body and in the fins. Refer to the species chapter for more details. The fact that some species show great variation in color as they mature has made their identification very difficult. This has resulted in many names being applied to what are actually different ontogenetic forms of the same species.

Fins: There are two basic types of fins in fishes, the median (unpaired) fins and the paired fins. The piranha has a larger dorsal fin followed by a small adipose fin. The anal fin and the caudal fin

Serrasalmus nattereri are caught by the local Indians for food.

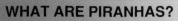

An 8 inch long *Serrasalmus nattereri* with its lips cut away to show its ferocious teeth.

PHOTO BY DR. HERBERT R. AXELROD.

Many of the Amazonian explorers catch and eat piranhas. They are usually gutted and fried in a pan. They are very plentiful and easy to catch with hook and line and a piece of raw meat as bait.

having evolved to rip pieces of flesh away from their victims. The teeth of each jaw, when closed, work rather like old animal traps. They interlock with each other to form a serrated cutting edge.

Scales: The scales of the piranha are of two types. The majority of scales covering the body are cycloid. This means they are of a basically round shape with smooth outer edges. You see only part of the scale, most being buried in the dermal layer of the skin. The second type are modified scales found along the ventral edge of the fish called scutes. In structure, the scales of a piranha are typical of all bony fishes. They are translucent, not colored as many non–aquarists and beginners may think, and they are loosely held in the skin, thus easily shed.

Digestive Tract: As is the case with all predatory animals, the intestines of the piranha are short when compared to that of

complete the unpaired fins. The caudal fin is variably indented to almost forked, as befits fishes capable of rapid movement in spite of their non–streamlined body.

The paired fins include the pectorals, which are situated just behind the lower part of the gill aperture on either side of the body, and the ventral fins. The ventral fins are found on the ventral sides, almost about the middle of the fish, and, because of their location, are also called abdominal fins.

Mouth: The mouth is bounded by fleshy lips. Its opening in piranhas is terminal to slightly superior, with the lower jaw protruding beyond the upper. This indicates that piranhas normally attack from below. The teeth may be in various arrangements, but are carried on the dentary bone below and the premaxilla above. They are relatively uniform in shape, and very sharp,

A 12 inch black piranha, *Serrasalmus niger* with its lips cut away to show its dangerous cutting teeth. This species is very dangerous.

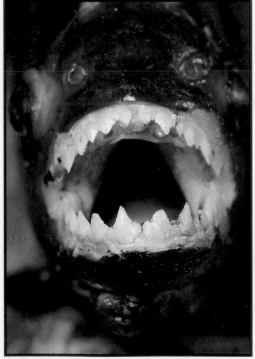

A mature specimen of *Serrasalmus nattereri* awaits unsuspecting prey as it hides behind a piece of wood.

herbivorous feeders, and the stomach is larger. This is because protein (flesh) is digested more readily than plant matter, whose hard cellulose walls require a longer time in the intestines.

Circulation: The circulatory system of the piranha is typical for that of most fishes. It is a simple single circulation. The heart is not four chambered as in mammals, but two chambered. Blood is pumped from the ventricle into the ventral aorta, thence to the gills via capillaries that go into each gill arch so that the blood can be oxygenated. It

adequate rather than good. In the murky waters of a river distance vision is hardly of use to a fish. It largely lacks binocular vision, but its field is good, with the eyes being placed laterally. The eyes can rotate very well so it is able to see anything approaching it from the front, sides, and rear.

More important to the piranha is its sense of smell, and its ability to detect any disturbances in the water. It is able to decipher the latter with remarkable ability, so it can sense a fish or animal that is floundering. Along the sides of its body are

PHOTO BY DR. HERBERT R. AXELROD.

Serrasalmus spilopleura.

is then picked up by more capillaries which feed the dorsal aorta, which transports it to the rest of the body.

Other capillaries gather the deoxygenated blood and transport it into the venous system (veins) which carry it back to the atrium of the heart. It passes via a valve into the ventricle to commence the circulation again. The heart is situated on the ventral part of the body just below and behind the gill arches, the safest position for it to be in.

Senses: The eyesight of a piranha is

a series of small openings that connect, via sensory cells, to the brain. This is called the lateral line, which also connects to the inner ear (fishes have no middle or outer ear).

The slightest vibrations in the water are picked up and amplified in the inner ear. In all cyprinids there is a special mechanism to assist in detecting changes in the water pressure surrounding the fish. This is a series of bones that connect the swim bladder to the inner ear and it is called the Weberian apparatus. Via these various mechanisms a piranha is very aware of all that is happening in its murky watery world.

It is because of a fish's great sensitivity to vibrations transmitted in water that the annoying habit of people tapping on the glass of fish tanks offends aquarists, who appreciate that this action can be distressing to these sensitive creatures.

Reproduction: Fishes reproduce in one of three ways. Some lay eggs that hatch outside of the body (oviparous), others lay eggs that hatch inside the female (ovoviviparous), while others have offspring that our nourished by the female and are true livebearers (viviparous). Piranhas belong to the first group, being oviparous (egglayers). More details are given in the breeding chapter.

Social Status: Piranhas are mostly schooling fishes, the size of a school varying depending on the type of species and environmental conditions. They roam along stretches of rivers and tributaries as opportunistic feeders taking whatever comes their way. During feeding frenzies it is quite normal for them to bite each other, but only when times are really hard will they actually become cannibalistic. Within the confines of a small aquarium they may attack each other, not so much because they are hungry (assuming they are well fed), but due to the pressures of stress brought about by the limited space they have.

However, although basically social, these fishes are just as capable of being solitary predators—much like a wolf is a pack animal, but is also a highly efficient predator when on its own. As a solitary hunter it will hover in reeds or near rocks and rely on stealth to catch its prey. Some species will actually swim within schools of their prey, suddenly taking one of these (or a piece of them) while the school is unaware what has happened. Piranhas will also prey on other piranhas, some being specialized to nip fins or scales of larger species. There is a tendency to regard the piranha as being a more important predator within its ecosystem than it actually is.

A school of *Serrasalmus nattereri* are safe from each other's attack because they are well fed. If they were to be left unfed, they would attack and eat each other.

PHOTO BY AQUA PRESS, MP AND C. PIEDNOIR.

AQUARIA, FILTERS, LIGHTS, AND HEAT

The first thing that you must understand if you have any thoughts of keeping piranhas is that you will need a large aquarium. This becomes even more important if you contemplate keeping two or more in a single tank. It is, of course, possible to keep a number of very(!) young individuals together in a moderate sized unit, but as they grow (and they can grow very fast) you would soon be faced with either having to house them in a larger tank, or having to obtain more tanks.

However, even overlooking the question of the tank size with respect to its life supporting ability, just as important is the fact that even young piranhas may start taking pieces out of each other. It is best to view these fishes as single tank occupants until a great deal of experience is gained with them. Other fish species (such as catfishes) may then be added. These might be able to cohabit with piranhas, but there is always the proviso that unless the aquarium is very large it is more than an even bet that sooner or later some problems will arise.

Individual specimens are often seen in quite modest sized aquaria, but this is not really the way to keep these fishes unless it is for short duration, such as at an exhibition. These are comparatively large fishes and need a home that allows them some capability of moving around. You should think in terms of an aquarium that has a capacity of at least 23 US gallons. The larger species will need tanks three to five times this size!

Not only will these aquaria take up quite a large amount of space in the average room, they will also be exceedingly heavy— more than enough to crash through any but the strongest floors. The average pet or aquarium store is unlikely to stock tanks suited to the larger species, so it will normally mean placing a special order. These are not species suited to the financially faint hearted when it comes to setting up the aquarium and obtaining examples!

AQUARIUM SHAPE & CONSTRUCTION

The best shape for an aquarium is the tried and tested rectangle. It displays the fishes best and is the most practical shape from a maintenance standpoint. It will also be a less expensive option.

With respect to its construction, you should ensure that it is constructed of the very finest materials. Large tanks hold a lot of water, which exerts considerable pressure on the glass panels. Any weaknesses may put you at risk of having the tank suddenly burst. The water will be all over the floor and will ruin your carpets—and this will not endear you to your neighbors if you live above them in an apartment. With these possibilities in mind it would be wise for the owners of a large unit to check whether or not they are well covered with insurance.

CALCULATING NEEDED TANK SIZE

Aquaria are sold either by their length or by their volume, the latter being the usual method in the US. You will need to know the volume in order to establish its weight when full of water, for calculating dosages of any medicines to be added to it, and for working out the size of the filter system needed to achieve the correct turnover of water. The surface area is important inasmuch as it determines the amount of oxygen that can be absorbed by the water, almost regardless of its volume.

This in turn influences the number of fishes that can be kept in that volume in the absence of auxiliary equipment. However, no doubt you will be using the latter, and the fact that you will probably only be keeping one or two piranhas means that it is unlikely you will risk overtaxing the oxygen retaining capabilities of the tank.

Nonetheless you should be aware of the accepted formulae for stocking rates in tropical(!) aquaria: Allow 75cm^2 (12in^2) of surface area for every 2.5cm (1in) of fish, excluding its tail. Using this formula we can take a sample tank, one with a length of 93cm (36in) and a width of 45cm (18in), and work out the size of a piranha it could house.

Surface area = L (93cm) x W (45cm) = 4,185cm^2

Divide by 75cm^2 = 55.8 units of surface area

Multiply units by 2.54 = 142cm (56in) of fish body.

A more rapid way to work out stocking levels is to divide the surface area by 30. Thus, in the sample given 4,185 divided by 30 = 139.5, which is close enough. In reverse, you can establish the total length of the adult fish body and multiply this by 30 to give the minimum surface area needed. The example tank, without additional aeration, would thus adequately suit any single piranha, and 2-5 of most species, without extra aeration, such as that provided via the filtration system. However, a 93cm long tank would give a 25cm piranha only a modest amount of room to swim in.

Even allowing for the extra oxygen needs of a large fish, such as the piranha, which has much body bulk, it can be seen that while surface area calculations may well be excellent for working out stocking levels of small tropical fishes, it is not quite as useful for a large species kept alone. With these fishes you must take into account the sheer size of the fish, so that it will have adequate space in which to move around.

AQUARIUM VOLUME

Apart from the other aspects of volume already discussed, of major importance is that it provides the total environment in which your piranha will be living. By the time the aquarium is furnished with a substrate, rocks, plants, and possibly filter equipment, the available swimming area remaining can be surprisingly small—depending on how much aquascaping has been done. As a general recommendation, you are always wise to obtain a unit that is somewhat larger than the one you had originally planned to get.

You can never have too much space in an aquarium, but you can certainly find that there is too little. It is also easier in many ways to maintain a larger unit than a smaller one. Water temperature, and its quality, tend to remain more stable the greater the volume concerned (which is why seas and oceans have less fluctuation in their temperatures than do rivers and lakes).

To calculate the volume of a tank, multiply its length times its width times its depth. Having established the volume you can easily work out the weight. You need not worry about the weight of the rocks and equipment because, from a practical standpoint, this will roughly approximate the weight of the water they displace.

Further, you will not be filling the tank to its capacity. Even allowing for the hood and its lights, the potential weight of the

PHOTO BY DR. HERBERT R. AXELROD.

The Berlin (Germany) Aquarium has a huge aquarium in which a large school of piranhas is exhibited. They are not dangerous when they are well fed.

water by volume will be a sound guide for consideration of the support strength you are likely to need to prevent it from going through the floor.

USEFUL CONVERSIONS AND CALCULATIONS

Volume = Length x width x depth. Example: 93x38x38cm = 134,292 cu. cm.

To convert volume to gallons: There are 3,785 cu. cm in a US gallon (or 231 cu. in. in a US Gallon). There are 4,537 cu. cm in a British gallon (or 277 cu. in. in a British gallon).

Example: 134,292 divided by 3,785 = 35.5 US gallons, divided by 4,537 = 29.6 UK gallons, and divided by 1,000 = 134 liters.

To convert US gallons to British (Imperial) gallons divide by 1.2, to convert British gallons to US gallons multiply by 1.2.

1 US gallon = 3.8 liters
1 British gallon = 4.55 liters
1 US gallon weighs 8.3 lb.
1 British gallon weighs 10 lb.
1 Liter weighs 2.2 lb
1 Kilogram = 2.2 lb.
1 US gallon = 3.8 Kilos
1 British gallon = 4.55 Kilos

From these various equivalents you can see that a 35.5 US gallon tank would weigh 295 lbs. This is equal to that of a very overweight person, though it might not look it. Such a tank would hardly be considered large by piranha standards. Given the weight factor you should consider where the aquarium is to be placed in your room, taking into account the numerous factors detailed in the following chapter.

AERATION & FILTRATION

The objective of aeration is to ensure that the water contains adequate amounts of dissolved oxygen for the fishes to breathe (via their gills). Filtration is to ensure that the water remains in a clean, unpolluted state. Although these two processes are separate entities, they can be combined in the filtration system. It is therefore not necessary to have a separate aeration system

Serrasalmus denticulatus is not one of the dangerous piranhas, but every piranha can bite, so keep your hands out of their aquarium!

PHOTO BY ANDRE ROTH.

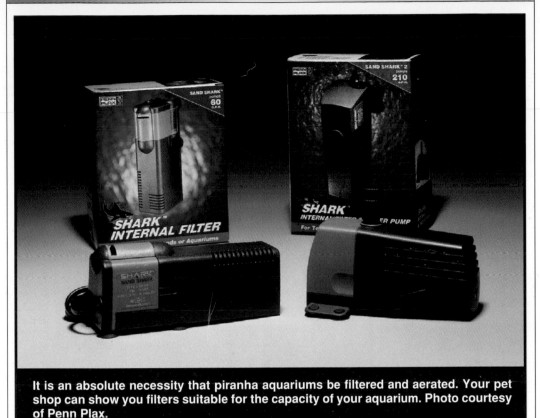

It is an absolute necessity that piranha aquariums be filtered and aerated. Your pet shop can show you filters suitable for the capacity of your aquarium. Photo courtesy of Penn Plax.

unless you wish to create esthetic effects from rising columns of bubbles.

You should, however, understand the principle of aeration. Air is passed from a small pump down a tube and exits via a special porous material, such as stone, to which it is attached. The rising column of bubbles burst at the surface. In so doing they disturb this and create mini waves. These effectively increase the surface area, thus that which is exposed to the atmosphere. This enables more oxygen to enter the water than would be the case if the interface was still. The rising bubbles on their way to the surface to release their air have little effect on the oxygen content of the tank. The size of the bubbles is regulated via the air stream from the pump, by valves or clamps on the piping, by the air stone size, or by a combination of these. Aeration has the secondary benefit of creating water circulation, by drawing water up behind the bubbles, thus helping to avoid temperature stratification in the deeper tanks.

FILTRATION

The filter system that you utilize in your aquarium is the main means by which you extract unwanted materials, gases, chemical compounds, etc., in solution or suspension from the water. The secondary method of their removal is via partial water changes. This keeps them in a diluted state, thus taking some of the work load from the filter system.

Filtration is achieved via one of three processes, which often act in more than one capacity.

1. Mechanical: This is effected by passing the water over or through any material that will prevent onward movement of solids. For example, if water is passed through synthetic filter wool, gravel, ceramic rings, glass chips, and their like, solid detritus will be trapped. Periodically the container holding the mechanical filter is removed and cleaned. The finer the filter, the more readily it will become "full" and slow down

the rate of water flowing through it. In a very large aquarium the mechanical filter may be of a two stage type—coarse and fine. This filter will also act in a biological capacity.

2. Chemical: This filter works on the basis that it attracts chemicals that are either in a dissolved state or are in very fine suspension so that they are able to pass through the average mechanical filter medium. The addition of other chemicals to the water (ion exchange resins) in order that these can combine with unwanted compounds to create a safe compound, also falls under the heading of chemical filtration. They are technically not filters but are grouped with them for practical reasons.

Charcoal is the most often used chemical filter as it adsorbs compounds and gases, thus rendering them harmless. Other examples are zeolite, and the various resins just mentioned. However, if chemical filters are not cleaned on a regular basis they may reverse their action and discharge the compounds back into the water. They thus become ineffective. Further, if medicines are added to the aquarium these filters must be removed otherwise they will remove, or negate the benefit of, the medicines.

3. Biological: This is actually a chemical process because it involves the conversion of ammonia to nitrites, then to nitrates, as discussed in the previous chapter. It is called biological filtration because living organisms are utilized. For these to survive they require a richly oxygenated surface on which to live. This can be the gravel substrate, rocks, and even the equipment. This form of filtration also acts as a mechanical filter. It is very important that biological filters are kept clean so that their oxygen supply remains high.

In the case of gravel cleaning is best accomplished by skimming the gravel with a tube siphon or gravel cleaner. If the gravel is removed during a major cleaning it should be washed in clean, cool to warm, water (never hot) with no chemicals added. These

may kill the beneficial bacteria. Likewise, when medicines are used check to see whether they are harmful or non destructive to the biological filter bacteria.

Filtration systems are available in many forms, from simple foam cartridges, through canister filters, to highly complex external units that may utilize ultraviolet light for killing microorganisms and protein skimmers for removing excess organic matter. The filter system may be internal, undergravel, or external. It may even be in a separate filter tank, and it may contain a heater for warming the water as well.

The latest external filters have bio-wheels to increase the biological action. These are said to be superior to the undergravel filters, which are loved or hated, depending on the experiences of various aquarists.

All of these filters work on the same principles. They draw water from the lower parts of the aquarium, where it will be the dirtiest and the least oxygenated. This water is then passed through one or more types of filter media before being returned to the surface of the tank via a tube or a spray bar. This return water agitates the water surface, thus increasing its oxygen content and allowing carbon dioxide and other gases to escape.

With respect to the needed flow rate of the filter, this will of course be dependent on numerous factors, such as the size of the tank and the number of fishes, thus the speed with which the tank water is being polluted. However, as a general guide you will need to pass the water through the filters about 3-4 times per hour. When purchasing your filter system check with your dealer that this will be achieved for the volume of water your aquarium holds.

The most popular filters at this time for your needs will be the external canister, power, or bio-wheel filters (which are also external). These have excellent turnover capacities and allow you to service them more easily than in-tank models, which also take up valuable space in the aquarium.

Undergravel filters are extremely efficient if they are set up correctly—much less so if they are not. As you want to minimize the number of times you may have to place your hands in the aquarium, it is perhaps better to use external filters.

LIGHTING NEEDS

Although you have a wide choice of lamp types, these ranging from tungsten bulbs through various forms of spotlights to fluorescent tubes, it is the last named that you should commence with. They cost less to run, are cool running, and are available in a spectral range suited to meet specific needs. Modern aquarium hoods are designed to accommodate these, some having built in reflectors as well.

Choose the spectral range of the lighting with care. Those that are excellent for encouraging plant growth will have a shorter life-span than will regular daylight tubes. They will also alter the natural colors of the fishes and the aquarium contents—but they will promote healthy plants. This may be a major consideration to you — remember that green algae is also a plant!

Regular daylight tubes will give a more natural lighting, but they are far less effective in creating esthetic appeal, or highlighting the colors of the fishes. If the illumination is too bright, this will encourage heavy algal growth and can make the unit look too "stark." A nice balance can be achieved by featuring one daylight tube and one of those that are biased toward the blue or red end of the spectrum.

The lights (lamps) you select for your piranha aquarium are very important for the well-being of your fish. Your pet shop can help you select the proper lamps. Photo courtesy of Penn Plax.

Unlike the situation with tungsten and spotlights, tube lighting wattage is related to the length of the tube. As this increases so does the wattage. There are different opinions as to how to calculate the amount of light (wattage) needed for an aquarium, so the following will be only general recommendations.

Fluorescent: 10 watts per 31cm (12in) of tank length, or 10 watts per 900cm^2 of surface area.

Lighting must take into account two aspects. One is subjective in that each aquarist's idea of what they perceive to be attractive will differ. The other is objective in that it must meet the needs of the plants if they are to flourish. These two realities allow for quite a range of experimentation in order to arrive at a satisfactory compromise. Bear in mind that the apparent life of a fluorescent tube will greatly exceed its effective life. This is because its beneficial rays will diminish over time and lose their value to the plants even though the tube is still emitting satisfactory viewing light. It is therefore wise to routinely replace tubes about every 6-9 months, depending on how many hours they are being used over a 24-hour period.

Piranhas live in regions that have approximately equal periods of night and day. However, you may find that this may be excessive and result in too much algal or other rampant plant growth, or the reverse, depending on the wattage's of lights being used. You must adjust this either way until, once again, a satisfactory balance has been achieved. Also, ensure that the water surface and cover glass are kept free of dust and dirt, and that the tubes are kept clean.

If not, much of the light's benefit will be lost to the aquarium.

In a very deep tank, fluorescent lighting will not penetrate to the lower depths sufficiently enough to provide good plant growth. Spot-lighting may be needed. However, when these are used you must be sure that there are sufficient shaded places where the fishes can avoid the intense brightness of these lights. If you wish to feature the more exotic plants, these are best added only after you have gained greater knowledge on the use of lighting, because this may be critical to their survival—as will the water conditions they need.

You should bear in mind that piranhas tend to prefer somewhat subdued lighting, as would be found in rivers over which there is a generous forest canopy, or shaded parts of the river.

HEATING

As with lighting, there are various ways in which a volume of water can be heated. We will restrict ourselves to combination heater/thermostats as these are by far the most popular. Be sure to purchase one of the well known name brands recommended by your pet or aquarium store. Do not obtain any from sources, such as supermarkets, or other places where there is no staff that can give you good advice on the brands they stock.

The best heater/thermostats will have a pilot light to indicate when the heater is working, and will have been preset so you can select the desired temperature before placing the heater in the water. Quality heaters operate at a very high degree of efficiency, and have a good life span. Even so, it is always wise to have a spare heater on hand just in case the one in the aquarium should malfunction.

In a large aquarium it is prudent to use two heaters, neither of which is capable, by itself, of taking the temperature beyond the desired level. At the same time, if one should fail the other should be able maintain the water at a safe temperature until the faulty one is replaced. If only one powerful heater is used it could raise the temperature to a dangerous, even lethal, level should the thermostat stick in the "on" position.

Deciding what the wattage of the heater(s) should be is subject to very diverse recommendations in aquarium circles. This is because there are many variables that must be taken into consideration. If the heater is very powerful it will be switching on and off continually, and heating the water at a rapid rate when "on". If it is under powered, it will be working for excessive periods, thus reducing its effective life. It may also be incapable of maintaining the needed heat if the ambient temperature of the room falls below its normal level. The larger tanks will maintain their heat for a longer period of time than will the smaller units. The critical factor with heaters is their ability to raise the temperature from that of the room to that needed in the aquarium.

Taking all of these factors into consideration, and assuming the room temperature will never fall 10°C below that required in the aquarium, you can work on the basis of 4 watts per gallon. If the room temperature might fall more than 10°, you should use 5, 6, or more watts per gallon, depending on just how cold the room gets. In actuality, if a room is subject to this sort of temperature drop overnight it would be very wise to place some insulation, such as cork, on the outer sides and rear aquarium panels to help conserve heat.

A 50-gallon tank will need 200 watts at 4 watts per gal. This can be provided via two 100 watt heaters spaced so as to give even heat distribution throughout the tank. This is more efficient than if a single 200 watt unit were used.

Even though the heater has a thermostat, do not rely completely on this. Always have at least one other accurate thermometer placed on or in the aquarium. Your pet shop has a selection ranging from external stick ons, through internal suction and free floating types—there are even microchip models.

It is very important that the temperature remains as constant as possible. Fishes react very badly to sudden changes of more than a couple of degrees within any 24-hour period. This is especially so if the temperature drops. This is another reason to obtain quality heaters, the quality comment applying equally as much to filter systems and most other aspects of the aquarium hobby.

Serrasalmus nattereri in this beautiful portrait looks almost harmless. Don't be fooled! These are dangerous fish both in Brazil and in your aquarium.

UNDERSTANDING WATER PROPERTIES

The fact that the average non–aquarist has little understanding of water properties is evident from the number of fishes that die each year as a direct result of this ignorance. Probably the best example of a lack of knowledge is seen in goldfish housed in globes that are totally inadequate as an environment in which to keep a fish. As a result, many perish before the owner seeks advice and obtains more suitable accommodations.

A piranha is far more demanding of its water properties than a goldfish, so you must understand their basic needs before even thinking of obtaining one of these — or any other fish species for that matter. Although it may seem that there is a lot to learn, it is not really difficult if you take each aspect one step at a time. Once you have set up your aquarium you will find that it is merely a matter of making routine checks to ensure that all is well. In the following text no assumption is made about your previous knowledge about aquarium keeping. Nothing of importance will be overlooked.

THE THREE WATER TYPES

Water can be divided into three broad types from an aquatic standpoint. These are salt (marine), estuarine, and fresh. Most fish species live in either pure fresh water or pure salt water, with only a relatively few being capable of living in or moving between these two major water types. Piranhas are strictly freshwater fishes. Their body fluids are more concentrated than that of the water they live in, the reverse being true of marine fishes. Through a process called osmosis, freshwater fishes are continually taking in water via their skin and gills and losing salt. To avoid the problem of over–hydration they drink little water and excrete a very dilute urine (between 5 and 12% of their body weight). Marine fishes do the reverse to avoid dehydration.

WATER TEMPERATURE

The temperature of a body of water has a considerable influence over its properties. It controls the amount of oxygen (and other gases as well) it can contain (the warmer it is the less oxygen it can hold). It influences the feeding habits of fishes—as the temperature of the water rises the appetite increases, until a point is reached beyond which they then decrease their food intake again. It influences breeding ability, growth, and resistance to diseases.

As a result of these many influences, fish species have evolved mechanisms to be able to live in water that displays a given range of temperatures. If they are placed in waters that have temperatures that are outside of their normal range they will quickly succumb to illness. Some fishes, for example goldfish and guppies, are very adaptable to temperature variables, as well as to other water properties, as long as these changes are very gradual. They are thus described as being very hardy fishes. Other fishes are less forgiving if their owner does not provide the needed conditions. Piranhas are among these fishes. The temperature range for most tropical species is 70-85°F (21-29.5°C), with 77°F (25°C) being an optimum level for piranhas.

ACIDITY & ALKALINITY (PH)

Water can range from very acid to very alkaline depending on where it comes from. If it is flowing over rather soft, easily dissolved, rocks it will tend to be alkaline due to the amount of salts the rocks contain. If it is flowing over hard insoluble rocks it will be neutral. If the substrate is composed of a great deal of organic matter the water will be acidic.

In order to determine the value of this property of water, aquarists use what is known as the pH scale. This is a measure of the number of hydrogen and hydroxide ions in the water. The scale runs from 1-14 with the mid point, 7, being called neutral—it has equal numbers of these ions. When there are more hydrogen ions in the water it becomes more acidic. When more hydroxide ions are available the water is more alkaline. A difference of one unit equates to a ten fold change in the acid or alkaline content of the water.

The piranha is native to waters that are rich in organic matter, so they are acidic. The pH range for most fishes is 5.5-7.5, with 6.6-6.7 being the optimum for most species. You can test water for its pH value using any of many kits available from your pet or aquarium store. Every kit comes with clear, easy to follow instructions. In the popular types you add a particular number of drops of a reagent to a sample of the aquarium water and compare the resulting color change with a chart that indicates the pH. You can obtain more accurate electronic indicators, but these are rather expensive.

The pH of water is affected both by the temperature and by other chemicals in the water. It will display a natural variation over any 24 hour period, so tests are best done at the same time of day on a regular schedule. The pH of water will affect the amount of oxygen the hemoglobin of the blood can take up, as will the amount of carbon dioxide, so you will appreciate that living in water is very complex and requires that at least the basic properties—such as pH—are kept as stable as possible.

WATER HARDNESS

As you are probably aware, water can range from very hard to very soft—in the former it is

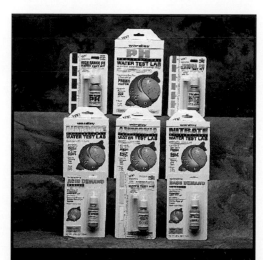

Monitoring the water in which your piranhas are maintained is very important. Your local pet shop will be able to supply you with various water test kits to measure pH, hardness and many other characteristics. Photo courtesy of Wardley Products.

hard to obtain lather from soap, in the latter very easy. Likewise, you will be aware that if the water is hard, kettles and pipes "fur" and will soon become blocked. As with pH, fishes have evolved to live in waters of a given hardness or softness. If the values are not correct for the particular fish, the delicate membranes of the gills are effected, as are the body cells. The result is obviously an inability to breath correctly, as well as other maladies.

As a guide, piranhas prefer water that is just slightly hard. There are various ways in which hardness can be expressed, the most popular being German degrees (dGH) and parts per million (ppm). The former measures the amount of calcium oxide in the water, the latter its calcium carbonate content. You can convert one to the other in the following manner (the less used Clark's (English) measurement is included for completeness):

One Clark degree = 14.3 ppm

One American degree = 17.1 ppm

One German degree = 17.9 ppm

Using ppm as the measurement, the following hardness states are generally defined:

0-100 ppm	= Soft
100-200 ppm	= Slightly to Moderately Hard
200-300 ppm	= Hard
300+ ppm	= Very Hard

The dGH recommendation for piranhas is 10, which is equal to 179 ppm. You need not worry if the hardness is not quite that suggested because fishes can tolerate a small variation as long as you maintain this as a steady constant once your fishes are established. This comment applies to many aspects of water properties. It is when these parameters fluctuate rapidly that problems will usually commence.

There are various test kits available from your pet or aquarium dealer by which hardness can be measured. Changing the hardness of your water is discussed in chapter 4.

CHLORINE

If you are using city water, you should be aware that it will have been treated with numerous chemicals in order to make it safe for you to drink. The concentrations of these chemicals varies from one locality to another— and from one period of time to another. Although these additives will not harm you they can, depending on what they are, be very dangerous to your fishes. Chlorine and chloramines are two prime examples of chemicals that are added to city water supplies that have adverse effects on your fishes. These can damage their delicate gill membranes and cause breathing difficulties.

Chlorine is easily removed by letting the water stand, whereupon the chlorine dissipates into the atmosphere. You can speed the process up by vigorously stirring (aerating) the water periodically, or by adding conditioning tablets

One of the best and most welcome aquarium accessories is the Automatic Water Changer which allows you to change the water, in full or partially, without carrying heavy buckets of water. Every pet shop has this invaluable tool. Photo courtesy of Aquarium Products.

obtained from your pet dealer, this latter being the most convenient way. Chloramines will require chemical conditioner treatment because they are far more stable than chlorine.

THE NITROGEN CYCLE

Another very important aspect of aquarium keeping is related to the process known as the nitrogen cycle. In this process, various waste products, such as fecal matter, decaying uneaten food, dead microscopic organisms, and the dead leaves of plants, all break down to form ammonia or ammonium. These are lethal to fishes even in very small amounts. By the action of bacteria they are converted to nitrites, which are no less toxic. In turn, the nitrites are converted into nitrates which are far less toxic, and which are utilized by plants as a source of food. The nitrobacter bacteria that convert nitrites to nitrates require a plentiful supply of oxygen and for that reason are called aerobic bacteria. These various bacteria are present in the atmosphere, but it takes them a long time to colonize the substrate and other surfaces in water. If fishes are introduced into an aquarium that does not have a large enough colony of these bacteria, the result will be that dangerous nitrites will be present. The fishes will be unable to breath adequately and may be

PHOTO BY DR. HERBERT R. AXELROD.

A *Serrasalmus eigenmanni* as a juvenile.

seen gasping at the surface as though the water lacked oxygen, which may not be the case. This situation is known as the "new tank" syndrome and is easily avoided if you apply correct techniques and are patient when setting up the aquarium. You can purchase bacterial starter cultures to speed up the nitrogen cycle, or you can dangle small slithers of meat in the water which will also help the process get started.

Aquarists may also transfer some substrate gravel from a mature tank to a new one so that the bacteria on the gravel help to establish a new colony. However, unless you are absolutely sure that the gravel is coming from a very healthy tank, this route is best avoided. There is always the risk that the gravel may contain the spores of pathogens (disease causing organisms) or the eggs of parasites. You can purchase test kits for ammonia, nitrites, and nitrates. But, due to the interrelationships of these compounds, you can assume that if the nitrite reading is zero, or very close to this, the other conversions are being effected satisfactorily. When an aquarium is first set

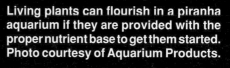

Living plants can flourish in a piranha aquarium if they are provided with the proper nutrient base to get them started. Photo courtesy of Aquarium Products.

up the nitrite levels will fluctuate widely, so you must wait until you are getting constant low readings before introducing any fishes. Even then, only one or two small individuals should be added, so that the bacterial colonies can build up in proportion to the amounts of potential pollution that the fishes, food, and so on, create. Ammonia will not be a problem if the water is even slightly acidic, which it will be for these fishes—it will be ammonium that is the danger. The reverse is true if the water is alkaline.

The whole process of the nitrogen cycle is made more efficient if you install a sound filtration system. This will greatly increase the aeration of the aquarium, and in particular that of the substrate.

METALS AND GASES

All metals, such as iron, copper, and zinc, can be dangerous at certain levels—especially copper. With this in mind it is always prudent to allow a faucet to run for a few seconds. This gets rid of the water that may have been standing in metal pipes. Likewise, avoid using rocks that may have traces of iron or other contaminants in them.

Carbon dioxide is a gas that is essential for healthy plant growth. It readily dissolves in water to form carbonic acid. Fishes release this gas via their gills as a byproduct of respiration. If excess carbon dioxide is present this will lower the amount of oxygen the blood cells can accommodate. Aquarists may introduce this gas into tanks in order to promote healthy plant growth, but should be aware of its danger to fish respiration when the level reaches 35 mg/l. Under normal aquarium conditions, the carbon dioxide level should not be something that will concern you. It is mentioned so that you are aware that fish respiration is complex and influenced by many factors due to the permeable structure of the gill membranes and the cells of the oral cavity.

UNKNOWN AND TRACE WATER PROPERTIES

In the same way that scientists do not know every single constituent of foods, every component of tainted water is not known, "tainted" water meaning water that is not absolutely pure and free of any additional compounds. The aquarist cannot know what compounds are in the water being used, or how they will combine or cause dissociation of other compounds.

A closed body of water, such as an aquarium, can suffer a build-up in the quantities of these unknown or trace chemicals to the point that they have a deleterious effect on the fishes. To avoid this possibility it is always recommended that you make regular partial water changes. This will at least ensure that these unknown "agents" are kept in a diluted state. About 20-25% of the water can be replaced every 2-3 weeks.

DETRITUS

The amount of dead or dying plants, together with the mulm and other detritus in suspension, are obvious indicators of how dirty an aquarium is. A dirty aquarium should be avoided at all costs because it is the precursor of all manner of problems. By the use of gravel cleaners, siphon tubes, and the regular cleaning of mechanical filters, you will greatly aid the efficient biological processes that are taking place. At the same time you will be denying most pathogens the sort of conditions they prefer in order to build up their numbers.

From the foregoing it is hoped that you will have gained a greater insight into the properties of water. You should now be aware that you cannot simply turn the faucet on, fill an aquarium, heat it, and then release fishes into it—not if you expect them to survive more than a few days at best. To a fish, water quality is as important to it as clean fresh air is to you. Indeed, a fish in the comparatively microscopic confines of even a large tank is less able to adapt to poor water conditions than you are to poor air. The water quality of your aquarium is the most important thing you need to understand in order to ensure that your piranha will live a contented and healthy life.

This beautiful *Serrasalmus gibbus* is rarely seen in the aquarium. It thrives under aquarium conditions.

FEEDING PIRANHAS

The piranhas have gained an evil reputation for being very greedy meat-eaters. However, there are more herbivorous piranha species than there are those with carnivorous diets. But even the herbivores are not beyond taking small fishes that will fit easily into their mouths. This is as true of goldfish and koi as it is of the more infamous piranhas. We will be looking at the carnivorous diet for it is the piranhas of this type that this book is essentially about.

In the wild, piranhas are both predators and scavengers—much like the hyena is in Africa. They are more than capable of killing any animal that lives in, or enters, their domain. However, their basic diet comprises small fish species, and those of any size that are sickly or wounded. They will also eat invertebrates, indeed, anything that comes their way when they are hungry.

What should be remembered with regard to any flesh-eating animal is that it does eat vegetation, but not in the direct sense. When it kills its prey the entire carcass is eaten. Within the intestinal tract of its prey will be vegetable matter in various degrees of breakdown. The predator thus consumes this partially digested vegetation and obtains valuable vitamins from it. These are added to those it obtains from meat and those that it is able to synthesize in its own body. The piranha also gains important minerals from the bones of its prey, so it has a completely balanced diet. When not feeding live prey to captive specimens, it is important that this need for a balanced diet is given major consideration.

OPTIONS FOR FEEDING PIRANHAS

You can feed your piranha in one of three ways. You can give it live foods, dead foods, or a mixture of both. Most aquarists do not like the idea of feeding one fish species to another, though a number of them use such a regimen. Fortunately, your piranha can survive very well on a diet that is no longer in the land of the living—if you prefer this method.

These fishes will hunt any smaller fish species placed into their aquarium. They will also consume those that are dead. They will eat worms of most kinds, as well as other invertebrates. Pieces of meat, poultry, and fish will be greedily taken, as will proprietary fish foods that are frozen, dried, flaked, or cubed, if these have a high protein base. Finally, you can make up mashes of various items, which can include eggs, meat, cheese and their like, and combine these with a pasty porridge to bind them together. The piranha will consume all.

In other words, these fishes can be fed much as any of the other smaller carnivorous fish species for aquaria, it being a case that the quantity will have to be much larger, and will therefore be more costly. However, taste is an acquired sense. You should not assume every piranha is a ravenous glutton that will eat just anything at all times. When their appetite is satiated, or nearly so, they will show disinterest in some foods, and bite only at favored items

If the notion of feeding live foods does not seem aberrant, you can purchase the unwanted surplus fishes produced by many aquarists, such as those who breed goldfish and guppies. Pet shops also sell these "feeder" fishes. Dead day-old chicks and small mice can also be fed to piranhas.

HOW MUCH TO FEED AND WHEN

Young piranhas need more meals per day than adults. This is especially so with fry, otherwise they will start devouring each other on the basis of the weakest gets eaten first. We will discuss the feeding of fry in the chapter on breeding. Juveniles and adults should be fed enough to satisfy their appetites. This is determined on a trial and error basis for each individual fish.

What you must try and avoid is polluting the water with more food than the piranha will consume at a single feeding. This means that you should feed small amounts at a time. Watch to be sure that all the food is being taken. When the piranha shows disinterest in further morsels, this is the time to stop. Note the amount you have given and repeat this at the next feeding. Over a couple of weeks you will establish fairly accurately what each piranha needs to satisfy its appetite, and thus remain in a healthy condition.

This is the pattern of their feeding habits in the wild. They may in fact go for days without food, then will gorge themselves as the opportunity presents itself. Some owners will imitate this pattern in their aquaria, feeding the piranhas only two or three times a week—but in larger quantities of course. If you prefer to feed them daily this is just fine.

The most important aspect is that the fish is receiving enough nourishment to maintain its health, and that the regimen is on a regular basis. The potential risk when

PHOTO BY DR. HERBERT R. AXELROD IN BARCELOS, BRAZIL ON THE RIO NEGRO.

This turtle was slaughtered and left at the edge of the river to bleed. It was attacked immediately by a school of piranhas which devastated the turtle in less than one minute!

With regard to the number of feedings, this is subject to varying views. An adult can manage quite well on a single meal given at a regular hour most convenient to you. A juvenile will be better off having two feedings per day. Carnivores are able to consume larger quantities at a time than can herbivorous species. They are then content to rest while that food is being digested.

fishes are not fed daily is that you may forget a meal, so they get very hungry. This would be a disastrous state of affairs if you have two piranhas living together. The possibility would be that one of them might start to view the other as its next meal!

It is important that you always observe your fishes when they eat. By so doing you will be well acquainted with the habits of each piranha. When a fish is ailing the first, and sometimes only, indication of this will be in its feeding habits. If you can pick up on any decrease or disinterest in its food you will of course keep a closer eye on the fish, and start to explore the reasons for this loss of appetite. You will be looking for further behavioral changes that would confirm that the fish has a problem.

FOOD SIZE AND SUPPLEMENTS

Although piranhas will snap at quite small foods, their size clearly suggests that they should be fed appropriate sized foods. Pieces of meat or dead fish should be large enough to allow them to utilize their razor sharp teeth to bite into them, rather than simply swallowing them whole because they were hardly worth biting!

When raw chunks of meat are fed, it must be remembered that these are deficient in certain needed dietary constituents. It is therefore wise to impregnate the meat with a suitable vitamin supplement. However, if you are feeding a varied diet that represents a good balanced diet, then additional supplements should not be needed. Indeed, your piranha can suffer from the negative effects of too many vitamins as much as it can suffer from a lack of them.

INFLUENCES ON APPETITE

Appetite is subject to various influences that you should be aware of. Possibly the most important of these is the water temperature. As the temperature rises toward the upper limit for the species, their appetite increases. Once past this limit, however, it will decrease. Conversely, as the temperature falls below that preferred by the species it will decrease, and eventually cease altogether—as will the fish if the temperature is that low!

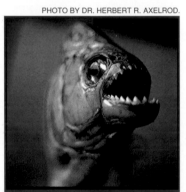

PHOTO BY DR. HERBERT R. AXELROD.

A close up of a stuffed but accurately portrayed piranha. The lips have been cut away but the teeth are real!

The age of your fish will also influence its feeding needs. A healthy growing piranha will consume more than a mature adult. It must put on a lot of muscle, as well as have adequate food for day-to-day activities, which are quite energetic in young fish. The adult needs only sufficient amounts to sustain its basic needs and replace any tissues worn out by day-to-day activity.

Breeding fish of both sexes will consume more than normal rations. This is because they will be in a heightened state of excitement, and will therefore be more active. A fish recovering from an illness will also consume more food because it must replace tissue that was broken down to provide energy while it was ill and not feeding normally. A stressed fish may eat more, or less, than a normal one depending on how it reacts to that which is stressing it.

In the case where two or more piranhas are sharing an aquarium you must not overlook the possibility that one fish may not get its share of the food because its tank mate(s) prevent it from doing so. Even piranhas are subject to the social influence of their conspecifics—especially if these are larger or simply more aggressive.

To say that nutrition is a science is only a partial truth as any skilled aquarist will tell you. It is also an art inasmuch that it is highly dependent on the owner's ability to observe and take account of the many factors that influence fishes in general, and individuals in particular.

If feeder fishes are used in the diet remember that piranhas are rather messy and although they will kill their prey, they may not always eat every part of it. Part of the head or body may fall to the substrate and be ignored. Also, bits of flesh will be in suspension in the water, so it is essential that regular cleanings take place to reduce pollution and prevent water cloudiness.

THE SUBSTRATE, DECORATIONS & SETTING UP

When you establish an aquarium you are doing far more than providing a sort of a "cage" for your animals. You are creating an entire world for them. Every effort should be made to include in it those elements of the wild habitat that will enable your fishes to lead a healthy and very contented life.

You will need a gravel substrate, various rocks and bogwoods, and a selection of plants. The arrangement of these, called the aqua-scene, should be such that the piranha has an open swimming area, and an area into which it can retreat for shade as well as a sense of security when this is needed. Other than these basic requirements, you will want to obtain various accessories for the setting up of the aquarium, and thereafter for generally maintaining it.

These items will include one or two plastic buckets (never metal), one or more lengths of plastic tubing to use as a siphon, a gravel cleaner, a glass scraper to remove algae, a few small pots to hold plants, a planter, inert plant weights, plant foods, various water test kits, and a good hand lens. You can also purchase murals that can be placed on the back and side panels of the aquarium to conceal the wall, or whatever may be behind the tank (such as pieces of equipment).

Finally, with respect to decoration, you can construct a "stage" at the back of the aquarium on which you can include various items that will give the tank the illusion of having greater depth. If this appeals to you, you must allow for this when positioning the aquarium. Now that you have listed your needs in general, let us commence by discussing these in more detail, and how to set up the aquarium.

Serrasalmus gibbus is called the "Golden Piranha" because of the golden color on its flanks and belly.

PHOTO BY ANDRE ROTH.

THE LOCATION

It is important that you choose the tank site with care. Very often this will mean a compromise that takes into account various factors.

1. The tank should be positioned such that it receives some natural daylight without being exposed to strong sunlight. The latter would interfere with the water temperature and encourage strong algal growth on the exposed panels. Piranhas do not like bright illumination.

2. It should not be where it will be subjected to cold drafts when doors are opened.

3. Avoid places where the human "traffic" is heavy and the fishes may be startled by the sudden appearance of a person. Stress created by this means can be a major precursor of illness. This is especially so with a piranha, which is actually a far more timid fish than you might think.

4. Select a site where it will be easy for you to service the aquarium with respect to partial water changes, cleaning, and general maintenance.

5. Avoid placing the unit close to heaters that will effect the temperature in the aquarium. As already discussed, rapid fluctuations in temperature is definitely a big negative where aquaria are concerned.

6. Choose a location where you can view your fishes with ease from the comfort of an armchair or sofa.

7. Double check that the location is well able to withstand the weight of the aquarium when it is filled with water. You can do this by stacking bricks or rocks of the same weight there, and spreading them over the same area that the tank will occupy.

THE SUBSTRATE

The floor of the tank should be covered with a layer of washed gravel that has a particle size of about one eighth of an inch. This provides a large enough surface area on which a good colony of beneficial bacteria can develop. If the substrate is of larger particle size it may provide pockets for uneaten food that will decay and increase pollution. If the particle size is too small it will be too fine for adequate water flow

Serrasalmus denticulatus from northwestern South America.

PHOTO BY ANDRE ROTH.

PHOTO BY ANDRE ROTH.

This fish acts like a piranha and schools with piranhas, but it might not be one; it hasn't been identified completely.

(and thus aeration) between the particles.

The depth should be about one inch at the front of the tank and rise to about three inches at the rear. This gradient promotes the accumulation of uneaten food and debris toward the front of the aquarium where it is more easily removed. Do not use any gravel that contains marble, oyster shell, or other calcium bearing material. You can utilize rocks or terraces to prevent the gravel from shifting toward the front of the tank.

ROCKS

As with the substrate, avoid using any calcium or metal bearing rocks—these would include marble, chalk, and dolomite. Over a span of time they will tend to make the water more alkaline and hard. Your best choices are granite, slate, basalt, lava, and hard sandstone. Choose an assortment of sizes from small through large, and those already smoothed by wear and with interesting shapes. You can purchase imitation rocks from your aquatic store. These look just like the real thing and are made from inert materials.

WOOD

This should be of the bogwood type, but never that which is rotting. This process consumes oxygen as a part of the decaying process. Woods that are not completely waterlogged will float, but you can weigh these down with rocks, or bind them with nylon string to a plastic base that is covered with gravel. You will never see the nylon string once a little algae has colonized the wood. As with rock, you can purchase synthetic woods shaped like branches, logs, and roots. These are heavier than water and totally safe to use.

PLANTS

A nice display of a few hardy plant species makes all the difference esthetically. All plants should be obtained from your aquarium dealer. Never gather them from the wild—you may inadvertently introduce pathogens to the aquarium. For piranhas, choose plants that are native to South America. These will include any of the broad leafed Amazon sword plants (genus *Echinodorus*). You need tall plants for the rear and sides of the tank, with maybe one or two short specimen plants for the foreground.

Because the piranha is a large fish, you should not overstock the tank with plants, but feature enough to provide a natural look, and provide clumps of plants that the fish can retreat among. Plants can be very demanding with regard to lighting conditions. This is why it is best to restrict the choice to hardy specimens recommended by your dealer.

Obtain a suitable fertilizer, and be sure to trim off any dead or dying leaves both before and after they are placed in the aquarium. As an extra precaution against the risk of introducing bacteria into the water via the plants, it is suggested that they first be disinfected using one of the proprietary plant disinfectants.

SETTING UP YOUR AQUARIUM DISPLAY

Setting up a piranha tank will take quite a few hours, so be sure you have allowed enough time. It can be done in two stages, the first being preparatory, the second the actual setting up. It is useful to first make sketches of the aqua-scene you visualize. This will help you avoid obtaining too many or too few of the decorations you need. It is also easier to move things around on paper than when they are in the actual tank. The latter should be restricted to changes in details.

In planning the scene, try to make it look natural by not having it too symmetrical. Large rocks can be placed off-center, or at one end. Logs and slate can be used to create bridges or cave-like retreats. Any internal equipment or its tubing can be discreetly hidden behind rocks or stands of tall pants.

The first practical job will be to test the tank for leaks by filling it. This is best done in the kitchen, or even outdoors, where a leak will not cause too much damage. You can place about one cup of salt into the water per every 20 gallons. This will kill most bacteria. Leave this overnight, then empty the tank and flush it generously with

clean water. The tank can then be placed in position. Before doing this check to make sure that the surface is as flat as possible. If any unevenness, however minor, is detected you can place a cork or polystyrene mat under the tank. It is important that there is no area that is unsupported and which would be subject to excess stress.

Next, all equipment and decorations must be cleaned. In the case of the gravel you can place this in a bucket of water and insert a hose into it. Let this run until the water is clear of all signs of cloudiness. Stirring the gravel will help free stubborn dirt particles. If a mural is to be added to the rear glass, attend to this when the tank is clean and empty.

Now the actual setting up can be done using the following guidelines.

1. If an undergravel filter is to be featured its plate must be installed first. It is very important that the water cannot bypass the filter. To prevent this, the edges can be sealed using an aquarium sealant.

2. Place a layer of gravel over the filter plate, or the glass tank bottom as the case may be. You can then add a layer of plant fertilizer to the gravel. Alternatively, you can restrict this food locally to where the plants are being inserted, especially if they are to be contained in pots or plastic bags (which might be wise if an undergravel filter is to be used). The current of water passing through the gravel to a filter can unduly disturb the plant roots if it is too strong.

3. Place the large rocks in position, trying to avoid any pockets under them by filling these in with gravel. Especially avoid small cave-like gaps under the rocks into which pieces of uneaten meat may be carried by the current. Once they become trapped they will rot and pollute the tank.

4. Insert any terracing (this can be done initially if no filter plate is to be used).

5. Complete the substrate, sculpturing it to your needs.

6. Fill the tank to a depth about one third full. To avoid disturbing the substrate pour the water gently onto a plate or other suitable material.

7. Insert the plants and any food for them. The plants can be secured in the gravel using plant weights or if they are potted by covering the planting medium with gravel. It is easier to work with the plants if there is water in the aquarium. Their leaves will float and not be in your way, or at risk of being damaged as might be the case if you insert them into dry gravel.

8. Now you can add the heater and filter tubing (or the filter itself if it is internal). Be sure that the heater element is not in the gravel. This will create uneven heating and

11. Make initial water quality tests and make notes on these. Fit the cover glass and canopy to the aquarium. It is best to let the water reach room temperature before you switch on the heater. But all other equipment can now be plugged into electrical sockets to check and see that they are in working order. Once the water is at room temperature, the heater can be plugged in. Check very carefully that the heater(s) are performing correctly.

Although with modern water conditioners you can very quickly add one or two inexpensive fishes to the aquarium,

Serrasalmus gibbus is not a sensitive fish and lives well under aquarium conditions. They may jump out of their aquarium, so keep it covered.

there is a risk that the glass of the unit will crack or shatter. Do not switch on any electrical equipment while you are in the setting up stage—this could be dangerous, or even lethal to you, if it were faulty.

9. Place the external filter into position, along with the air pump, if one is being used.

10. Fill the aquarium to about 1-2 inches from the top. Add water conditioners to remove the chlorine and chloramines. Now is the time to use your long-handled planter to make any minor changes in the plant arrangement. If you wish, you can add nitrogen cycle starter cultures, or small slithers of meat on a string, so the needed bacterial colonies can be encouraged to start.

it is wise to wait at least two weeks before adding a piranha. This gives the water at least some time to mature and build up the bacterial colony needed to convert the nitrites to nitrates. It can take months to build up a large bacterial colony in a large aquarium.

You will find, initially, that the nitrite reading will fluctuate considerably, so you must wait until it has peaked and dropped and is constantly at zero or very close to this. Likewise, the pH reading will vary depending on the time of day the water is tested, so do this at the same time of day on a regular schedule.

If the pH or hardness levels are not as required you can obtain resins from your dealer to adjust these to desired values. Peat in the filters will increase acidity, chalk in it will increase hardness.

ADDING THE PIRANHA

Only when the water conditions are just right, and especially only when the temperature is constant at about 77°F should you purchase and introduce the piranha. There are three things to take into consideration. First the bag in which the piranha was transported (if it was a bag) should be floated on the surface to let its water temperature equate with that of the aquarium water. Next you should carefully open the neck of the bag and allow some tank water into it so that the fish gets a "feeling" for the new water. Finally, you can open the bag completely and let the fish swim gently into the tank. The whole process can take from 20-40 minutes. Do not "pour" the fish into the tank. This will stress it badly. It may panic and damage itself against the glass or rocks.

You are cautioned in all of your dealings with these fishes that while most of them will not be aggressive, all of them can inflict dangerous bites, so must be handled with the greatest respect at all times. Of course, very young fish of two inches or less will hardly be able to inflict more than a tiny bite, but you should learn to respect them from the outset.

ROUTINE CLEANING

Once the aquarium is up and running it must be routinely attended. This means removing debris from the tank, cleaning the filters, and removing excess algae from the viewing glass, rocks, and equipment. Test the water on a regular basis—minor fluctuations in pH and hardness will not be a problem, but those related to nitrates are indicative of whether or not the nitrogen cycle is being effected adequately.

Partial water changes should be made every 21 days or so at which time 25% of the water can be exchanged. Be sure to heat the added water so that it is at the required

Serrasalmus denticulatus are dangerous in many ways. Submergible heaters with cables loose in the water are in danger of being bitten by piranhas.

PHOTO BY ANDRE ROTH.

This species has been sold as a piranha. When it starts eating plants instead of other fishes, you know it's not a piranha!

temperature before it is placed in the aquarium.

SAFETY PRECAUTIONS

There are two safety considerations. One is related to the electricity, the other to the piranha. Never (!) place your hands into water while the electrical equipment is plugged into a socket. With respect to the fish, it is wise not to risk getting bitten, even though your piranha is apparently placid.

One way to work at chores in the tank, and do so safely, is to obtain a sheet of Plexiglas the width and height of the tank and drill a number of small holes into it (the holes allow it to be moved in the aquarium with greater ease). It should be tall enough that the fish cannot swim over it. By using this as a divider you can restrict the fish's movement so that you can reach into the aquarium without any risk that your pet will decide to try and snack on your arm or bite your fingers, or nip at them in fright. The alternative is, of course, to remove the piranha to a smaller holding tank. This is the way to proceed when a major cleaning job is to be undertaken.

As for the actual catching process, nets must be avoided as these fish can easily bite holes in them. In any case, rough nets may also damage the piranha's scales and fins. The gentlest, and safest, way to move a piranha from one tank to another is by the use of a plastic trap or bucket into which the fish is herded using a small net.

In the event a piranha of reasonable size should somehow flip out of a bucket, exercise extreme care when recovering it. When flipping on a carpet a piranha will panic and bite madly at anything and everything. Place an empty bucket near them and as gently as possibly scoop them into this, quickly adding some aquarium water.

THE TRUTH ABOUT WILD PIRANHAS

The piranha is hardly alone among animals that have gained fearsome reputations as being the most dangerous creatures in their domains. Consider gorillas, sharks, wolves, snakes, tarantulas, and tigers, just to name a few. Few animals are as timid and retiring as gorillas, and most sharks would flee, or show little more than curiosity, at the sight of a human. The reliably documented accounts of wolves attacking humans could be counted on the fingers of one hand, while only a few snakes represent any threat to humans—and these commonly only attack when provoked or startled.

This is not to say that the piranha and the other creatures mentioned are not dangerous. It is simply that their danger has been blown out of all proportion. News reporters, together with TV and movie producers, are little concerned with things that are not regarded as especially dangerous in the day-to-day lives of people who live with these creatures. That doesn't sell their products. However, if a fish that most people know nothing about can strip a man to bare bones in seconds, now that is something else!

Matters are certainly exacerbated if a well respected person states that this or that animal is highly dangerous to humans and all others it comes into contact with. Never mind if that person never actually studied the animal's habits to establish any basis for the believed facts he or she was stating. Once a legend has been built, it can be very difficult to dispel, especially if there is in fact an element of truth on which that legend has been based. This is the case with piranhas.

THE RISKY LIFE OF THE PIRANHA

The first way to bring perspective to the truth about a piranha is to look at certain realities concerning its own ability to survive in the wild. If these fishes were indeed such ferocious killers it would follow that there would be few other fishes or other creatures living in waters where it abounds. It would have hunted them out of existence, in which case, by now, most piranhas would then have eaten each other! The fact that hundreds of other fish species live in the same waters as piranhas would strongly suggest that these fishes are successful enough in avoiding being eaten so that the piranha is unable to decimate their populations.

The piranha is not a predator that reigns over its domain with impunity. It is itself a prey species to many other animals that live in the same waters—such is the complex web of life. Granted, it is a prime predator, much as the lion and tiger are, but they, too, have no "golden passport" to survival in their domain.

If the largest of the piranhas were to carelessly pass in front of the jaws of a waiting crocodile or caiman, it would quickly find its reputation meant nothing to these animals! It would rapidly be just another morsel to these reptiles. Every year many thousands of piranhas end up as meals to these creatures.

Similar numbers end up in the bellies of river dolphins, while even more thousands fall prey to river turtles and otters. Otters! But aren't these mammals like us? That's right, and there are other non-fish or non-reptile species that have no aversion to taking a few piranhas as a meal, including large herons, eagles, and other fish-eating birds.

Now if this isn't bad enough for the piranha, most of its own prey species will actually decimate the piranhas before they become large enough to eat their prey. Millions of piranha eggs and fry will never live for more time than it takes for some quite small fishes to come along and gobble them up, just another snack in their own quest for food.

So, getting by as an adult piranha can be

PHOTO BY HARALD SCHULTZ.

This Karaja indian caught this *Serrasalmus nattereri* for his dinner.

quite difficult at the best of times, and the odds are heavily stacked against it reaching maturity in the first place. If you then add to the equation the hundreds of thousands that are caught each year by native fishermen, the piranha needs all of its ferocity and reputation in order to hold its own within its domain! It must also be born in mind that its prey species don't just stay put and allow themselves to be eaten. Some are much faster swimmers than the piranha, and quickly put distance between themselves and the piranha (or a school of them). The prey, too, usually have very sensitive detection devices and can detect schools of predators (piranhas) moving toward them in the water.

Other fish species, when approached by a piranha on a one-to-one basis, will turn toward it and stand their ground. When this happens the piranha may have "second thoughts" about attacking—much as an individual lion is easily dissuaded from attacking a water buffalo that turns to face it.

The result of these realities is that the piranha has to really work hard to survive— just like all the other inhabitants of the rivers and lakes in which it lives. A balanced equilibrium is thus maintained.

THE THREAT TO HUMANS

The foregoing should have dispelled the notion that the piranha is anything more than just another of life's problems to most creatures that share its domain. The piranha is to them just another threat and/or just another potential meal. As a threat it is no more dangerous than a crocodile, a dolphin, a turtle, an otter, a bird, a snake, or any of hundreds of other animals that will make a meal of them if the opportunity arises. Some fish species are even more at risk to certain of these animals, or to other fish species, such as catfishes, than they are to the piranha.

This brings us to the threat to humans by these undeniably dangerous fishes. There is an infinitely higher risk that a piranha will be killed by a human than there is of a human being killed by a piranha. There is a much higher risk that a human will be killed, or mauled, in piranha infested waters by other

fish species, reptiles, or mammals, than there is from direct danger at the mouths of these fishes. In terms of hard facts, your chances of being attacked by something in the jungles or rain forests of South America are such that you would be safer swimming with the piranhas than staying on land! Each year hundreds of South American natives are killed by venomous snakes—but documented evidence of deaths by piranhas is almost impossible to come by.

It must, however, be conceded that if a school of piranhas did attack a human there would be little evidence to document! It is this little word "if" that is enough to perpetuate the legend of the piranha. Even the most knowledgeable expert on these fishes would not be foolish enough to state that there would be no risk to a human entering piranha infested waters.

It comes down more to a case of the odds against a person being attacked, and under what conditions would these odds start to change such that one would be very well advised not to take them. The chances of a human being attacked are remote at best. There are sound reasons for this. Mammals generally, and humans especially, are not aquatic, thus not among the normal prey species of these fishes. As a result, a piranha has better things to do with its time than to be unduly concerned by the sight of a human in water. Like most sharks, lions, or other creatures, it may show interest in a human because it cannot be sure how secure its own life is. It is able to detect that the human is larger than itself, and thus may be dangerous—so it will keep its distance. It will check the odors and the sound waves (pressure waves) for any indications of distress or blood. If these are not evident it will move on looking for more easy-to-take natural prey whose habits it is far more familiar with.

HOW THE ODDS CHANGE

The river-bank natives of piranha habitats know when it is and isn't safe to enter the water. They know the piranha will become excited by the smell of blood, and that this

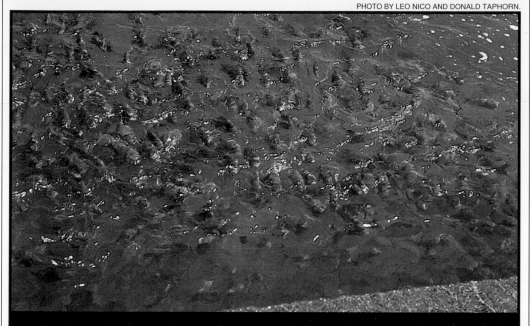

PHOTO BY LEO NICO AND DONALD TAPHORN.

A school of piranhas, *Pygocentrus* or *Serrasalmus notatus* in a feeding frenzy.

will attract any piranhas lurking in the immediate vicinity. They know that if an animal or fish is in distress it will thrash about in the water, and that this, too, will attract these fishes. And they know that certain parts of a river may be favorite hunting grounds for piranhas. These fishes will tend to congregate at such places. It is likely that they will be making regular kills there, so will often be in an excited state.

They know that if a stretch of water has dried out or has become cut off from its main flow, the piranha will exhaust the water of prey fishes, and eventually become very hungry. This will drive them to be less cautious and to be more likely to "test bite" any potentially edible item.

Under these conditions one or more of the more bold piranhas will approach ever closer, then eventually snap at the human. Once the first bite is taken and blood is flowing, the school will go into its feeding frenzy. Its natural fear or disinterest of the human will instantly vanish. Once this state is reached, unless the human is in very shallow water, the chances of him or her coming out alive would be all but zero, depending, of course, on how many

piranhas were present.

The natives have ascertained all of these facts over many years. They may never have seen a person killed in piranha infested waters, but they were educated from the cradle that these realities were truths handed down to them by their parents, and to them by their parents, and so on. They see sufficient evidence of these truths in their daily lives—-partially consumed fishes, baited meat, or bites on other natives from the careless handling of a netted piranha.

They and their children can swim and thrash without concern in the shallow waters near their village. They know that as long as they do not have open wounds the piranha may come, but will then go away again when no scent of blood or sense of distress is established. So regular are these routines that the piranha will ultimately not even bother to come too close.

When crossing deeper stretches of rivers the natives will do so slowly and without attracting undue attention to themselves, though wide and deep rivers will normally only be crossed via canoe—why push your luck!

A head on view of a young *Serrasalmus nattereri*. His teeth are always showing and his eyes are pitched in such a way that he has binocular vision, a rare characteristic among fishes. Most of them can only focus both eyes on objects in a distance.

From the foregoing you will see that these fishes are no more dangerous to a human than is the crocodile that will lay basking along the banks of the same rivers, or the anaconda that may be swimming in the river, or the stingray that lays motionless on the sandy substrate. That it is capable of accomplishing everything its evil reputation tells us it can is not in dispute. It is the likelihood of it doing so to the average informed traveler of regions where it lives is where the truth has been bent and twisted to the degree it has formed a circle!

For all of the truths given in this discussion, the piranha will still maintain its place as one of the most feared animals we can think of. The reason is that with most other animals having similar notorious reputations, we also believe that there would be some chance we could avoid death. Maybe a stick would keep them at bay, or we might have a gun, or could climb a tree—or maybe even jump into a river. But if piranhas attacked in numbers there simply would be no chance of escape and survival. That is a sobering truth!

BREEDING PIRANHAS

The breeding of piranhas is still very much in its infancy, since only a few species having been bred, and these usually in the very large tanks of public aquariums. The species bred so far are *S. spilopleura*, *S. gibbus*, *S. rhombeus*, and possibly *Pygocentrus nattereri*.

The reasons for this dearth of success are not surprising. Any attempts to breed these fishes should not even be contemplated unless one has a tank of at least 100-300-gallon capacity. This immediately places breeding well out of the reach of the average aquarist. There is then the fact that the sexes, with but one exception, are not readily identifiable externally. This means that a number of them must be kept in order to try and discern, by behavior patterns, which are possibly a true pair.

Even having obtained a pair and supplying them with a large enough aquarium, it has to be hoped that they will be compatible. This is by no means certain. Some time may also be required (which may be a year or two) before they are ready to reproduce, and only then if all conditions are to their liking.

Finally, even if a pair spawned it would be a costly undertaking to raise even a few of these to maturity unless you had more large tanks for rearing purposes. Piranha fry, even a few days old, are quite ferocious toward their siblings, and have no qualms in adding them to their daily menu. If other adults are sharing the same tank, these too will soon devour the youngsters. Given these rather depressing realities, the following information will complete your knowledge on these fishes, and provide some data and hints for those who are in a position to attempt to breed their piranhas.

Hiroshi Azuma stunned the aquarium world with his spawning of *Serrasalmus nattereri* in Japan many years ago. He lost many females when they became egg-bound. By dissecting them, Azuma found thousands of small, ripe eggs.

PHOTO BY HIROSHI AZUMA.

EGGLAYING

Piranhas are oviparous fishes, meaning they are egglayers, the eggs hatching outside of their body. Even within this method of reproduction there are different techniques used to ensure that a percentage of the eggs survive and develop into fry. Some species are egg scatterers, the currents taking the eggs away from the parents who would otherwise eat them.

Some fishes are egg buriers, placing their eggs in the substrate. Some are egg depositors, carefully fixing the eggs to plants or rocks where they are guarded by the parents. Piranhas are in the group known as nest-builders, though there are scatterers among them as well. The former prepare rough nests from leaves or depressions they make in the substrate. Here the eggs are laid and guarded by one or both parents— predominantly the male. This care of the eggs and fry seems rather out of place, given the ferocity of these fishes. But those piranhas that do defend their offspring do so with the same level of aggression that they show in their day to day predatory lives.

In spite of this parental care, if other fishes share the same tank, which is not advisable with breeding pairs, many eggs and fry will be eaten while they are still very small and unable to defend themselves, which they surely will do once they have reached a few inches in length.

BREEDING PREPARATION

Before piranhas can be bred they must be in superb physical condition—well fed, contented, and stress-free in their accommodations. They are thus best kept in pairs so that there are no other fishes to bother them.

Inducing breeding is not yet fully understood, it being more a case of "if you see the signs they must be ready." Raising the temperature a few degrees may help induce spawning, as may the addition of a little fresh water. A pair will commonly

The breeding pair of *Serrasalmus nattereri* prepare to spawn by clearing the area. They move the small stones and chew up the vegetation to make a suitable spawning nest.

Once the breeding pair of *Serrasalmus nattereri* have prepared their spawning site, they rub against each other and release huge quantities of eggs.

swim together and the male will probably start to display a darkening of his colors in a very short time span. The pair will commence nest preparations by biting away pieces of vegetation, moving small rocks, and fashioning a depression at a chosen site. It is therefore essential that they have suitable plants, which should include those that will readily hold the eggs, such as Java moss, or peat in which depressions can be made. The male will drive the female around the tank in an effort to guide her to the nesting area. He may take pieces from her fins (and body), and vice versa, so courtship in these fishes is conducted at much the same level of violence as most other aspects of their lives!

Eventually, she will come to rest in the spawning area and he will approach her from the side in order to fertilize as many of her eggs as he can. This ritual will be repeated a number of times until all the eggs are shed.

EGGS AND THEIR CARE

The number of eggs laid is very variable, but within the range of 700-4,000. They are deposited as a sticky mass so that they will retain their position in the nest (if of this type). Alternatively, the egg scattering species, such as *S. gibbus*, will simply deposit their eggs at random around the spawning area.

If egg scattering is observed, it would be wise to remove the parents as chances are they will readily eat them (and fry if the eggs ever get to hatch). In fact, even with parents that protect their eggs it may be prudent, with a first spawning, to do likewise, or to remove most of the eggs to a safe place for hatching. This is in case the parents become nervous and decide to devour their brood. At the next spawning you could always allow them to look after most, or even all, of their offspring to see how things go.

It is advised that you treat the water with a suitable disinfectant, such as methylene blue, from your pet shop so as to minimize the risk of fungus attacking the eggs. However, this usually happens only to the eggs that are infertile, the healthy ones usually proving very resistant to fungus and parasites, assuming that the water is clean and not polluted.

If eggs are hatched away from the main tank the suggested initial temperature is 77°F, which should be raised by 3-4 degrees when the eggs hatch.

REARING THE FRY

Once the eggs hatch, which will be anytime after 2-9 days depending on the species and the water temperature, the fry will soon begin feeding on newly hatched brine shrimp. They rapidly progress to small worms, and if not given enough food, they will just as rapidly attack each other!

It is essential, in order to minimize cannibalism, that each fry has at least one gallon of water—thus 50 fry will need a minimum tank size of 50 gallons. In reality, because of the numbers of fry that hatch, and the speed with which they grow—about 2.5cm (1in) a month—it is almost inevitable that within the average hobbyists' tanks most will perish for one reason or another, usually due to lack of space and/or food.

After about five months the growth rate starts to slow down a little, and by eight to ten months most are losing, or have lost,

A close-up of *Serrasalmus nattereri* eggs which adhere to the spawning substrata. The developing embryos are clearly visible. Most of the thousands of eggs released by the female were successfully fertilized by the male.

PHOTO BY HIROSHI AZUMA

A two-week old embryo of *Serrasalmus nattereri* with its yolk sac almost entirely absorbed. The fry is about 1 cm in length (there are 2.54 cm to an inch).

their juvenile coloration. These remarks are of course based on just the few species in which breeding has been observed, so it remains to be seen if what has just been said is reasonably typical for the genus as a whole.

Once a spawning has taken place, the pair may spawn again within two or three weeks, but this may prove to be an unwanted happening if you already have one batch of fry that you are trying to raise.

KEEPING RECORDS

Given the scarcity of breeding reports within this group of fishes every spawning is something of an achievement. This being so, it behooves breeders to maintain diligent records of any successful spawnings so that this can be disseminated among other breeders. The sort of data that should be recorded is as follows:

Observations on behavioral patterns that preceded courtship.

Color changes in the fish.

Water conditions.

Plants and other decorations in the aquarium.

Age of parents (if known) and their size.

How long they had been together, and were others in the same tank.

Observations on the placement of eggs and any nests that were prepared.

Hatching time.

Foods supplied.

Growth rate.

Notes on behavior of the fry, and the development of their colors and markings.

This information can be supplied to hobbyists through clubs as well as through articles that can be offered to aquarium magazines or scientific journals.

THE PIRANHA SPECIES

Before discussing the various piranha species you are likely to choose from, there are three other subjects that will be of interest to you. These relate to the legality of owning any of these fishes, your responsibility to your pet, and the derivation of the name piranha.

PIRANHAS—THEIR LEGAL STATUS

Before purchasing a piranha you are advised to check its legal standing in both your state and area. Many states forbid the ownership of these fishes. Even where they may be kept statewide there may be local ordinances that forbid them. The reason is that in the federal and state departments there is a fear that if these fishes were to be released into local rivers or lakes they might become established, thus have a devastating effect on indigenous species. There is also the perceived danger to humans.

Such releases are most likely from people trying to dispose of unwanted pets. Now you might think that pet owners would never do this—sadly you would be very wrong. Within all pet hobbies there are a small number of people who should never be allowed to own any animal. They are totally irresponsible, uncaring, and move from one pet to another on a fanciful whim. They are the scourge of pet hobbies. They are the sort that dump dogs, cats, potbellied pigs, and other pets into local parks to get rid of them. They also release unwanted cage birds, and will release surplus stocks of fishes into ponds and rivers. While the chances of a few released piranhas being able to establish populations in habitats alien to them is remote in the extreme, it would be equally irresponsible of serious hobbyists to say this could not be possible. Wild populations of non–indigenous species of fishes, birds, and mammals residing now in the USA, and other countries, are testimony to this fact.

A PIRANHA OWNER'S RESPONSIBILITY

Before you even purchase a piranha you should carefully examine your reasons for wanting one. If it is to impress friends, or simply to watch it devour defenseless fishes, these are very poor reasons and the desired effect will not last long. As a responsible owner you should consider the reality that the small youngster(s) you obtain will soon become much larger, and will cost more to feed. If you are not prepared to invest a substantially larger sum of money into relocating them in a large tank, what will you do with them? Do not assume that a public aquarium or a pet shop will be prepared to take them from you—even at no cost.

If these outlets are not interested in your now-too-large piranha, you must be prepared to contact tropical fish clubs to see if they have members who will take the fish. This is entirely possible. However, if all these avenues fail, the only(!) responsible option left is to have your vet painlessly destroy the fish.

Do not think that releasing them into the wild is being considerate toward your pet. This is ducking responsibility. Such a released piranha would be doomed to a miserable existence that can only end in starvation, illness, and slow death, unless another predator devoured it, which is eventually what would probably happen.

THE NAME "PIRANHA"

The common name of this group of species has its derivation in the languages used by South American Indians that have known the fish as long as they have had a language. Their own languages have been subject to hybridization resulting from the effect of successive waves of other Indian tribes that have invaded them, and by words introduced by Spanish and Portuguese colonists. Locally, piranhas are known

Various fishes have been sold as piranhas. Here are some which are NOT piranhas and are not dangerous:
1. The Hatchetfish, *Carnegiella marthae* prefers eating small insects. 2. *Piaractus brachypomum* really looks like a piranha, but it isn't. 3. A full grown *Colossoma macropomum*. 4. *Colossoma macropomum* juvenile. 5. *Mylossoma paraguayensis* is a vegetarian. 6. *Mylossoma duriventre* is a vegetable eating fish. It doesn't eat other fishes. 7. *Mylossoma aureum* is a vegetarian as are all *Mylossoma*. 8. *Mylossoma aureum* juvenile.
All of these fishes can be kept in the same aquarium but they will eat live plants so only use plastic plants, rocks and safe driftwood.

under many different names according to the habits of the fishes, dangerous or less so, and by their colors.

Let us start with the correct pronunciation. It is not "peranna" as most English speaking people will say it. It should be pronounced "Pee-rrahn'-ya", with the accent on the "rahn" and a rolled "r", though few English speaking people can roll the "r" as do the Spanish and Portuguese.

In the general hybrid Amazonian language of patois spoken by many natives, and derived from the Tupi tribe, pira means a fish. Rahna, tanha and sanha, depending on locality, mean tooth. Thus the Pira-rahna is the toothed fish, and when shortened by the English it became piranha.

However, some early explorers translated it as meaning "scissors" fish, overlooking the fact that these appliances were probably named for the fish, not the reverse. When the first Indians saw scissors the cutting action reminded them of the teeth of these fishes, so scissors came to be known as piranha. Historically, and to this day, the teeth of these fish were in fact used for various cutting tools by the Indians, so the early error by explorers is easy to understand.

Without going into all of their derivations, the following are just some of the other names used in South American countries for these fishes, some of which indicate whether they refer to those known to be dangerous, or those regarded as not so dangerous. You may see them appearing from time to time in the literature.

Caribe: Venezuela. Dangerous species. Named for the Carib Indian tribe, a very cruel tribe of marauding conquerors.

Chupita: Brazil. Dangerous species.

Pacu: Non dangerous piranhas and related species.

Palometa: Bolivia and Uruguay. Dangerous species, though the term means "little dove." The word piranha in these countries is, ironically, applied to the less dangerous species.

Pana: Peru.

Perai or Pirai: Guyana. The most dangerous species.

Piraya. Brazil. A corruption of piranha used in certain areas.

Pirambeba. North and Eastern Brazil. Non dangerous species.

Piranha-verdadeira: Brazil. The true dangerous piranha.

Rodoleira: Brazil. General name.

Umati: Brazil. Indian name for piranha.

THE SPECIES

Exactly how many species of piranha there are is open to much debate in zoological circles. This is because some species have been labeled such on no more than color and size differences, and are based on limited numbers of specimens. Large numbers of specimens are fundamental to any authoritative classification. It is always possible, as has been illustrated in fishes, birds, and other animal groups, that what was considered for a long time to be a species was no more than an immature example that displayed juvenile size and color differences. Piranhas show a tremendous range of colors, which change as they mature, so errors from this aspect are easy to make.

Sexually dimorphic examples (where the sexes are distinguished on the basis of external appearance) have also been labeled as different species, as have geographic color variants. It is therefore entirely possible that some of the following species may at some future date be found to be one and the same. It is also quite probable that some species remain to be identified and described scientifically. Others listed may prove yet to be subspecies.

The subgeneric status of these fishes has been ignored here because this taxon is invariably changed continually by taxonomists. The species are arranged alphabetically rather than by distribution (as is normal) so you can more readily refer to them.

Sizes are maximum approximates for mature specimens, head and body only (without tail). A number of species have no common names as they are not as yet well known enough in the hobby to have been given

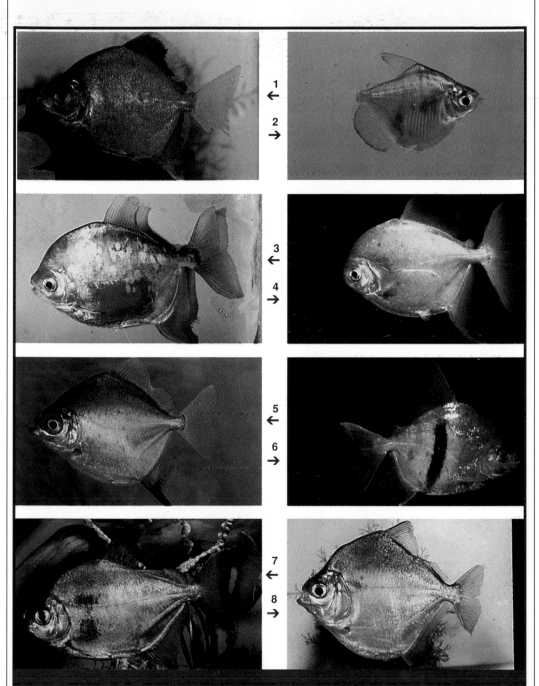

These fishes are usually sold as piranhas, but now that the importation of piranhas is banned in most civilized countries, the tables have turned and the piranhas are now called by non-piranha names on export documents. 1. *Myleus pacu* is the name of this so-called metynnis. The name *pacu* is the indian name used in Brazil. 2. *Myleus micans*. 3. and 4. *Myleus rubripinnis*. This may be the most popular of the *Myleus*. 5. *Myleus ternetzi*. 6. *Myleus schomburgki* is the most expensive of the *Myleus*. 7. *Metynnis argenteus*. 8. *Metynnis luna*.

them. Common names have no scientific standing anyway, becoming established solely by convention of their use.

The name following the species name is its author and following that is the date the species was first described. If the author's name is in parentheses this indicates that the species was originally placed in another genus.

Descriptive text, other than for color and markings, has been restricted to those species you are likely to be able to obtain and where the species is well documented and therefore of interest to hobbyists.

There are currently four genera of "piranhas" (*Pristobrycon, Pygocentrus, Pygopristis,* and *Serrasalmus*), with a fifth (*Catoprion*) generally included with the group by aquarists although not a true piranha. However, the piranhas are undergoing a revision and no doubt their classification will undergo many changes before it is finished. For that reason, even though scientists have generally accepted the breakdown of the genus *Serrasalmus* into the genera mentioned in the text, aquarists still use the name for all of the piranhas, which is reflected in the captions.

Catoprion mento (Cuvier, 1819)
Wimple or Winged piranha
Venezuela, Guianas, Brazil, Bolivia. 14cm (5.5in). Although not in the genera of true piranhas, the wimple (meaning banner) piranha has become progressively more popular with aquarists. It rarely exceeds 10cm (4in), but its fin-nipping habits mean that it's best kept in a single species tank.

It is named for the elongated rays of its anterior dorsal and anal fins. Color is silvery with a red opercular spot, a black base to the caudal fin, and brick red in the anal fin. The species breeds well in captivity.

Pristobrycon aureus (Spix in Agassiz, 1829)
Golden piranha.
Venezuela, Brazil. 36cm (14in). Caribe dorado = savage gold. Color is an iridescent mixture of olive and gold, the body covered with very small dark spots. Not regarded as an especially dangerous species, it is nevertheless not popular.

Pristobrycon calmoni (Steindachner, 1908)
Dusky piranha
Brazil. 23cm (9in). The dorsal area of this rather bland piranha is gray to black. A dark blotch present behind gills. Some red in the anal fin. Body is silvery with faint black spots. Occasionally available, but not popular.

Pristobrycon striolatus (Steindachner, 1908)
Venezuela, Guyana. The profile suggests a non dangerous species. Color is dark above, sides silvery, and red into the paired and anal fins. The base of the tail is black banded.

Pygocentrus cariba (Humboldt, in Humboldt & Valenciennes, 1821) Red-bellied piranha
Venezuela, Brazil. 25cm (10in). This is another species that is somewhat similar to *P. nattereri,* which also has the common name red-bellied piranha applied to it. It is also an aggressive and somewhat unpredictable fish in an aquarium. Its distinctive shoulder spot and more fiery red color should help differentiate it from its much more popular cousin. *P. notatus* is a synonym.

Pygocentrus nattereri (Kner), 1860
Red Piranha, Red-bellied Piranha, Natterer's Piranha
Venezuela, Guiana, Brazil, Paraguay. 25cm (10in). The mature *P. nattereri* has a silvery iridescent body richly speckled with green-blue. The throat and underbelly are red of varying intensities, while the nape is grayish. In contrast, juveniles are not unlike *S. hollandi* with their spotted bodies. Colors vary greatly as the species matures.

These are all fishes of the genus *Catoprion*. There are three species. The usual species with the relatively shorter anal and dorsal fins is called *Catoprion mento*. It was first described in 1819. Dr. Axelrod described *Catoprion* "Geryi" from the Mato Grosso. It looks like *Catoprion mento* except the fish has a double longest ray in the dorsal and anal fins. A third species from the Pantanal of the Rio Paraguay drainage has extremely long dorsal and anal fins and Dr. Axelrod has called this *Catoprion* "Paraguayensis".

The adult bulldog-like build indicates quite clearly that this is a dangerous fish, possibly the most dangerous for its size in its wild habitat. It is also by far the most popular in the aquarium hobby, being much smaller than the similar looking piraya. It is a well-established breeder in aquaria.

Pygocentrus piraya (Cuvier, 1819)

Brazil. 53cm (21in). This very large piranha is dark-colored, ranging from Olive-brown to almost black, but with uneven silvery spots showing through and some red under the throat. It is definitely one of the most dangerous species, requiring a very large tank with very few companions! Not popular.

Pygocentrus ternetzi Steindachner, 1908

Paraguay, Argentina. 25cm (10in). Similar to *P. nattereri*, and may even wind up being a synonym of that species, but current thought is that the southern populations should be considered a valid species (*P. ternetzi*). It is another of the dangerous species in its natural habitat.

Pygopristis antoni Fernandez-Yepez, 1965

Venezuela. Caribe palometa = savage dove. Basic color silvery with black spots on the dorsal area. Some red in the paired fins and lower jaw, also in the anal fin. Now considered a possible synonym of *P. denticulatus*.

Pygopristis denticulatus (Cuvier, 1819)

Venezuela, Guianas, Brazil. 20cm (8in). Caribe palometa = Savage dove. This species has a silver color with some faint dark spots. The paired fins are yellow through red, this becoming a dark ochre to red with a black ending on the large anal fin. Not a highly dangerous species, nevertheless it should be treated with great respect. Its teeth are five cusped. The male of this species has a pronounced extension of the anterior rays of the anal fin when compared to that of the female—assuming this fin is fully intact, which is not always the case with this group of fishes.

Serrasalmus altuvei Ramírez, 1965.

Venezuela. Caribe azul = savage blue. The back is well humped, the lower jaw more upturned. Color silvery with some blue on flanks. Pinkish hues on underbelly. Dark vertical markings

Serrasalmus brandtii Reinhardt in Lütken, 1874

Brazil. This silver piranha with some yellow and brown in the anal and paired fins, is one of the non-dangerous species. The tell-tale signs are the large eyes, the less pronounced mouth, the smaller (but still very sharp) teeth, and the slim, compressed body.

Serrasalmus eigenmanni Norman, 1928

Venezuela, Guyana. The upper body is a mixture of olive and steel blue, the flanks being silver changing to white on the underbelly. Breeding pairs, as in a number of species, become much darker in color. Some red in paired, and anal fins. Upper body sports large dark spots. Although said to be non dangerous, it is better regarded as midway between the two types. Body rhomboid.

Serrasalmus elongatus Kner, 1860 Pike piranha

Venezuela, Brazil. 25cm (10in). This species is one of the least piranha shaped, being rather elongated. The color is basically all silver. It is a scale or fin nipper of larger fishes, but will of course attack and swallow smaller species. It is within the "non dangerous to humans" category.

Serrasalmus gibbus Castelnau, 1855 Golden piranha

Brazil, Peru. 31cm (12in). Named for the golden color of its flanks and underbelly, the dorsal surface is dark, being shades of blue. As with most piranhas, there is an iridescence to the scales. It is a dangerous species occasionally available to aquarists. Possibly a synonym of *S. rhombeus* (Linnaeus, 1766).

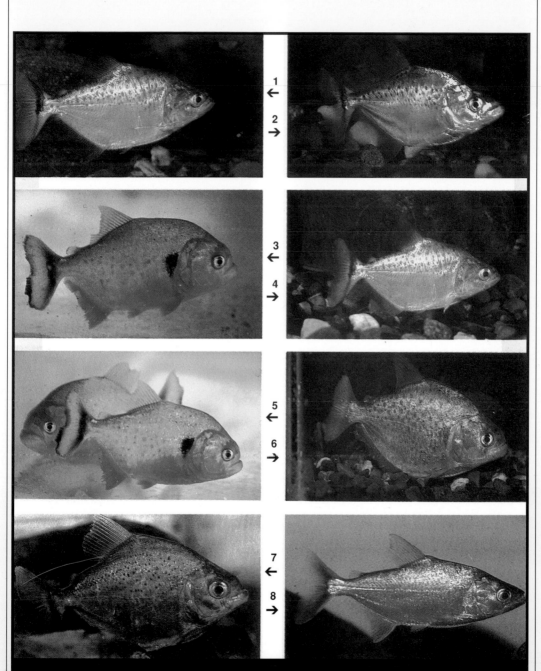

These are all REAL piranhas. They are dangerous both in the wild and in the aquarium. They do not attack humans in nature unless they are starving. In the aquarium they attack your hand because they are threatened. 1. *Serrasalmus eigenmanni*. 2. *Serrasalmus eigenmanni*. 3. *Serrasalmus notatus*. 4. *Serrasalmus eigenmanni*. 5. *Serrasalmus notatus*. 6. An unidentified *Serrasalmus*. 7. *Serrasalmus striolatus*. 8. *Serrasalmus elongatus*.

Some real and some imitators. 1. *Metynnis maculatus* is a very attractive fish with what looks like a red gash on its belly. This is strictly a plant-eater. 2. *Metynnis hypsauchen*. 3. *Serrasalmus gibbus* is a dangerous piranha. 4. *Serrasalmus sanchezi*. 5. *Serrasalmus spilopleura*. 6. *Serrasalmus antoni*. 7. *Serrasalmus denticulatus*. 8. *Serrasalmus striolatus* which looks like a *Metynnis* but has the teeth of a piranha.

A group of the rarely seen piranhas include many of the common ones but from hard-to-reach areas. *Serrasalmus nattereri* is a very variable piranha which soon should be separated into a dozen species when some aggressive splitter studies them. 1. *Serrasalmus elongatus* is a lake species which is very elongated. 2. *Serrasalmus hollandi*. 3. *Serrasalmus nattereri*, a juvenile. 4. *Serrasalmus nattereri*, sub-adult. 5. *Serrasalmus manueli*. 6. *Serrasalmus nattereri*, an adult. 7. *Serrasalmus rhombeus*, so named because of its shape. 8. *Serrasalmus serrulatus*.

Serrasalmus hollandi Eigenmann, 1915
Holland's piranha
Brazil. 15cm (6in). Being one of the smaller species, *S. hollandi* is suited to the aquarium hobby more than most species. It is in the non dangerous category. The ground color is silver to blue-brown, depending on the light reflections. There are distinctive dark spots of varying intensity. Some red in the fins, most noticeably in the anal. Tail almost transparent, with a dark base. Will become very dark in color with age—and when breeding. The shape is not unlike that of *S. rhombeus*.

Serrasalmus nalseni Fernandez-Yepez, 1969
Venezuela. This species is another of those that feature dark spots on its body. With red in its fins time may prove it is not a good species but a synonym of an earlier named species.

Serrasalmus niger (Schomburgk in Jardine, 1864)
Black piranha
Venezuela, Guianas. 36cm (14in). Although this large dark to black piranha has a much more unsavory reputation than *S. rhombeus*, it is considered to be the same species by some authorities. It is also regarded as being very unpredictable in its nature when kept in aquaria, so it is not very popular.

Serrasalmus nigricans Agassiz in Spix & Agassiz, 1829
Brazil. 25cm (10in). Somewhat similar to *P. nattereri*, but smaller and lacking red on the body and in the fins.

Serrasalmus pingke Fernandez-Yepez, 1951
Venezuela. This piranha has an elongate body and is considered a synonym of *S. elongatus*. It is called caribe pinche, meaning minion.

Serrasalmus rhombeus (Linnaeus, 1766)
White piranha, Spotted piranha
Venezuela, Guyana, Brazil. 46cm (18 in). This very large piranha is easily distinguished from *S. hollandi* by its larger size, the caudal and ventral fin colors, these being black edged in this species, and by the larger number of dark spots covering its body. Not dangerous—this applying to its danger level in the wild, it is still capable of taking a sizable piece from your finger if you get careless!

Serrasalmus serrulatus (Valenciennes, 1849)
Venezuela, Brazil. 41 cm (16 in). Not an especially colorful species, being a mixture of dull olive and silver with some dark horizontal blotches on the dorsal surface. Although very large, it is not considered to be dangerous to humans in its habitat. It is not popular in the hobby. Its status is also uncertain.

Serrasalmus spilopleura Kner, 1859
Dark banded piranha
Venezuela, Guianas, Brazil, Paraguay, Argentina. 31cm (12in). Like so many piranhas, the dark banded piranha, named for the terminal band on the caudal fin, displays sufficient variation in colors as it matures to make it difficult to describe precisely. The dorsal surface is dark, being olive green to brown. Flanks silvery. It has variable amounts of red around the throat and onto the anterior abdomen. The eyes are red. It breeds well in captivity. Regarded as being not dangerous to humans, but with sufficient doubt to be treated with great respect.

Other Genera
Species that are similar to the piranhas in other genera of Serrasalmidae are often called pacus or silver dollars. They include *Myleus*, *Metynnis*, *Mylossoma*, *Utiaritichthys*, *Acnodon*, *Mylesinus*, *Piaractus*, and *Colossoma*.

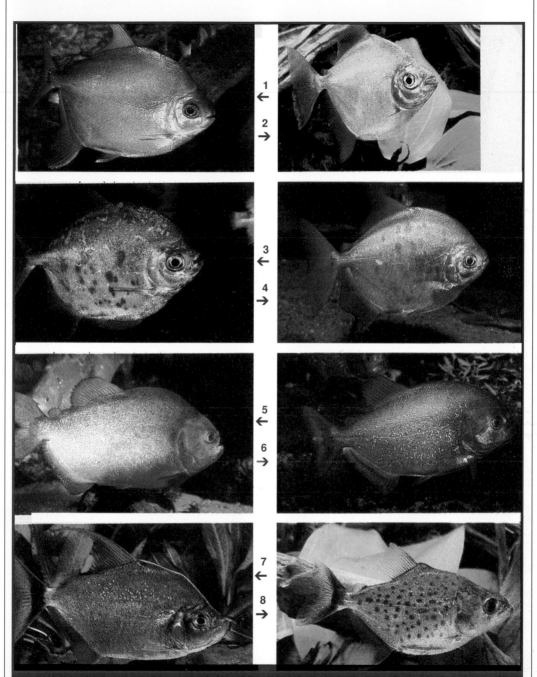

One of the ways to check your fish to ascertain whether or not it is a piranha, is to look at the distance between the end of the eye and the end of the gill cover. Piranhas always have a least two eye diameters between their eye and the end of the gill cover while the other fishes have less. 1. *Metynnis*, unidentified. 2. *Myleus rubripinnis*, a juvenile. 3. *Myleus rubripinnis* variant. 4. *Myleus rubripinnis* adult. 5. *Serrasalmus nattereri*. 6. *Serrasalmus nattereri*. 7. *Catoprion mento*. 8. *Serrasalmus hollandi*.

The black metynnis as it is sometimes called, has also passed for the black piranha. Actually it is neither. This vegetarian is *Colossoma macropomum*.

KEEPING PIRANHAS HEALTHY

Piranhas are remarkably hardy fishes in some ways, yet very delicate in others. Likewise, they are very aggressive in their nature, yet can be both exceedingly timid and nervous. For example, while they seem to recover remarkably quickly from even deep wounds, they can soon succumb to sudden drops in temperature.

They may readily become involved in battles with their own kind, or with prey, yet they can become badly stressed by excessive light, noises, and disturbances to their environment. Because they are not the most easy fishes to handle, it is altogether better that problems are avoided rather than treated.

PREVENTIVE MEDICINE

Most of the problems aquarists, indeed all pet owners, are faced with can often be traced back to a number of causes that could have been avoided by preventive husbandry techniques. These are associated with the following subjects.

1. Correct stocking levels
2. Adequate hygiene
3. Sound nutrition
4. Appreciation of stress factors
5. Prompt action when problems are detected
6. Quarantine

Without attention to these matters, all of the volumes devoted to the diseases of fishes will prove of little value, because problems will simply occur again and again. This chapter, therefore, targets these vital areas rather than cataloging diseases that are better covered in larger works where details and treatments can be explained more fully than would be possible here.

It must always be remembered that problems are rarely attributable to a single cause. Often, a combination of factors based on those listed will be present, each being contributory to the problem. Conversely, as you correct one area of management, this may directly or indirectly correct another.

STOCKING LEVELS

Lack of adequate space is a prime problem in many aquaria. Put another way, many aquarists, especially those new to the hobby, overcrowd their tanks. They assume that as long as there is sufficient oxygen to supply the needs of the fishes all will be well. Alas, this is rarely the case.

For one thing, every fish needs a given amount of space around it and adequate space in which to avoid having to be continually on the move. When this is not available the result is a build-up of tensions in the community. This dramatically increases stress and the risk of diseases resulting from this.

The communities more active state, coupled with the number of fishes, increases the carbon dioxide content, and few owners monitor this aspect. With a piranha, space is all important because these fishes are very aware of each other's destructive dental capabilities. If they are forced to coexist in a limited space the only result can be constant fighting and extreme stress.

If you ever start to think that if two are nice, three would be better, try telling yourself two may be nice, but three could be disastrous. This is likely to be the truth of the matter with piranhas unless you are prepared to invest in a much larger tank.

HYGIENE

It is really easy to introduce a pathogen (disease causing agent) into an aquarium. But it can prove almost impossible to remove it, and then only after a considerable cost has been paid in one form or another. Bacteria may gain access to the water via rocks, gravel, equipment, accessories, plants, the food, your hands, and of course via the air surrounding the tank.

You cannot avoid a degree of risk because it is inevitable, but you can minimize this by continually making sure that everything is cleaned before it is placed into the water, and every time you take something out. Foods should be fresh and stored under cool, dark, dry conditions. Be sure to routinely clean the aquarium, removing debris and uneaten foods on a regular basis.

NUTRITION

A varied and balanced diet is the cornerstone of good health. If you start to take short cuts in the quality or quantity of food you offer your piranhas, you are heading on a downhill path that can only increase the risk of illness. With piranhas there is the added factor that if two or more fish are living together, any shortfall in their diet will invariably result in an increased rate of aggression, and maybe the eating of the smaller or weaker individual(s) by the larger, stronger ones.

This being said, you must make sure that the food supplied is eaten, otherwise it will create another problem, that of polluting the water with its own attendant problems.

THE STRESS FACTOR

Stress is a major ballplayer in the causes of diseases. It reduces the immune system's ability to function at full capacity, thus it lowers resistance to even the most insignificant of ailments. The problem of identifying stress factors is that they are not always the same for each animal—what upsets one may not do so to the next.

However, as a general guide it can be assumed that the more natural the action that is denied the animal, the greater the stress factor. Piranhas always have adequate space in the wild, so lack of it will cause stress. They are able to keep given distances from each other in the wild. If this is not possible in your aquarium, this too will be a major stress factor.

They are nervous, indeed timid, fishes that have lots of hiding places in the wild, so should have similar hiding places in an aquarium. They can easily avoid bright sunshine in the wild, so should not be

A school of piranhas lives in peace in a large aquarium providing they are always well fed.

PHOTO BY DR. HERBERT R. AXELROD

Serrasalmus nattereri spawning.

subjected to it in the aquarium—or should have ample shaded places where they can avoid it. No fishes like light entering from the sides of their environment—it makes them nervous. You should thus screen the back and sides of their aquarium which at least limits the laterally entering light to the front viewing glass.

Avoid sudden noises and sudden changes in light intensities. Be sure that in a community situation the fishes are all of the same size. If not, the smaller ones will be badly stressed by the closeness of larger, potentially predatory conspecifics. Try to avoid free-for-all feeding techniques—feed each piranha its own meal at opposite ends of the aquarium so as to avoid confrontation or bullying.

PROMPT ACTION TO PROBLEMS

If you suspect one of your fish is ill, do not wait to see how things develop over the next few days. Chances are high that they will simply get much worse. The fish must either be treated in the aquarium, or it must be removed for individual treatment in a hospital tank. An added problem with piranhas is that if one of a small community of these fishes becomes ill it is less able to avoid attacks by its fellows and may suffer badly as a result.

Make notes on any problems, both clinical signs and those that are behavioral, then seek advice as quickly as possible. The sooner treatment is effected, the sooner a recovery will be made. Remember, if medicines are to be added to the main tank, you must remove carbon and other filter materials that might adsorb them. Also, you may have to slow down the filter flow rate to allow the medicines more time to work.

The down side of this is that it may adversely effect the beneficial bacterial colony in the substrate, so only slow things down for short periods. This fact also underscores the benefit of never overcrowding an aquarium, thus placing a heavy strain on the filter system. Check to see whether or not the medicine is "friendly" to substrate bacteria.

In a failed breeding attempt, this *Serrasalmus spilopleura* lost parts of its fins. Usually such problems resolve themselves without medication or treatment. But if they fungus, immediate action must be taken to save the life of the fish.

PHOTO BY DR. HERBERT R. AXELROD

PHOTO BY DR. HERBERT R. AXELROD.

Serrasalmus gibbus **is a magnificent fish and is very dangerous both in nature and in the tank. It is, however, very sensitive to medicines and chemicals put into the aquarium water. If one becomes ill, treat it in a separate tank.**

QUARANTINE

Once you have an established aquarium, a golden rule should be that no additional stock is introduced to this unless it has passed through a quarantine period to minimize the risk of introducing pathogens into the tank.

This means that you must have a spare tank, albeit a smaller one, in which new arrivals can spend 14-21 days while you check them out. This tank can double as a hospital tank. When setting up a quarantine tank, the water should be adjusted to the water temperature and chemistry of the seller's tank. It can then be adjusted over the quarantine period to match that of your display aquarium.

While the new arrivals are in quarantine you can observe their eating habits and adjust these to your own regimen. As a general precaution against parasites, it is recommended that you add about one teaspoonful of salt per gallon of water. A good hand lens would also be worthwhile so that you could carefully study your new pet to check to see that it is free of any obvious external parasites. Furnish the tank sparsely, but include some places it can retreat to. Use plastic rather than real plants, and dark glass marbles can be used as a substrate. A simple filter, and possibly an air stone, should ensure adequate filtration and aeration.

RECOGNIZING A SICK PIRANHA

A fish will either show behavioral, clinical, or no signs of ill health. Those that show no signs of a problem of course are impossible to treat because the first you know of a problem is when you find a dead piranha, or its remains if it has been partly devoured. The latter is worse because if it was ill, and was then eaten, the pathogen may have been transported to a new host.

Behavioral Signs: The fish will be listless, may hide far more than is normal, may make darting movements through the tank, may be seen rubbing against rocks, gasping at the surface, swimming at an unusual angle, show disinterest in its food, or lay on the substrate with its fins clamped close to its body or fully extended.

Clinical Signs: Any swellings or lumps; cloudiness of the eyes; cottonwool like

The most rare and most elegant of the piranhas is the black piranha, *Serrasalmus niger* from Brazil.

PHOTO BY DR. HERBERT R. AXELROD.

growths anywhere on the head, body, or fins; white, yellow, black, or other spots (other than those which are features of the species); rotting fins that are streaked with blood, undue swelling of the abdomen; blood streaked fecal matter; bulging or sunken eyes; emaciation; holes anywhere on the fish; scales standing away from the body; excessive mucus on the skin resulting in a dulling of the colors; ulcers; gray color to the gills (instead of a healthy pink), or inflammation of these.

Wounds and missing parts of fins are quite common in piranhas, given their lifestyle, but ordinarily these will not cause too much of a problem, and they regenerate quite quickly. However, the danger here is that they can be the site for parasitic or bacterial invasion, which in turn can lead to a secondary infection. This is far more likely if the water is not clean and of the required quality and temperature.

TREATMENTS

For many minor problems a raising of the temperature by a few degrees may be effective, as might the addition of salt to the water (as mentioned), and possibly at a higher concentration—2-3 teaspoonfuls per gallon. Other treatments will utilize any of numerous modern drugs that have been produced for tropical fishes in recent years.

However, before using these medicines it is important that you are sure what you are treating, otherwise the medicine will not be effective: it may even aggravate the situation! Veterinary advice—or that of an experienced aquarist or well established dealer—is therefore suggested.

If, following a treatment, the problem recurs, the chances are high that conditions in the aquarium are not satisfactory. Alternatively, the spores of some pathogens are very resilient to treatments.

The solution may be a total breaking down of the aquarium, the destruction of the plants, the replacement of the rocks, or a heavy disinfecting of these with household bleach, and careful cleaning of the filter system and everything else that is in contact with the water. Such action is, fortunately, not often needed, but the thought of having to do this should prompt all aquarists to pay that extra attention to general husbandry techniques.

Finally, it should be added that when purchasing fishes it really does pay to carefully check the tanks of those selling the fishes to ensure that their standards of management are of the highest order. Do not go for the cheapest fishes because a dealer who invests the time and money in maintaining high standards simply cannot compete with merchants who are able to cut prices simply because they have poor standards of care and nutrition.

PHOTO BY DR. HERBERT R. AXELROD.

These piranhas were collected in the Rio Aguaro, Venezuela by Dr. Axelrod. They were identified as *Serrasalmus hollandi* by Dr. Gery and as *Pygocentrus striolatus* by Dr. Fernandez-Yepez.

INDEX

Page numbers in **boldface** refer to illustrations.